P9-BVC-816

AN EVOLUTION IN UNDERSTANDING OF THE PROBLEM OF ALCOHOL

A History of College Idealism

By

HARRY S. WARNER, L.H.D.

THE CHRISTOPHER PUBLISHING HOUSE
BOSTON, U.S.A.

Library of Congress Catalog Card Number 66-15393

PRINTED IN
THE UNITED STATES OF AMERICA

DEDICATED TO

LEIGH, VIRGIL, LOGAN
AND MY WIFE FLORENCE

Who lived through life the ideals
of their college days

BOOKS AND PAMPHLET PUBLICATIONS

By Harry S. Warner, L.H.D.

BOOKS

Social Welfare and the Liquor Problem, 1908-1916. Second Edition completely rewritten; seven printings.

Prohibition in Outline, co-author with F. Ernest Johnson, 1927.

Prohibition, an Adventure in Freedom, 1928.

Why Prohibition? Will It Work? A syllabus to promote all around discussion.

The Liquor Cult and Its Culture, 1946.

An Evolution in Understanding of the Problem of Alcohol, A History of College Idealism, 1900-1965.

PAMPHLETS

"A Constructive Equivalent for War."

"Winning Orations in the Public Speaking Contest of the Intercollegiate Prohibition Association": each two years, 1907, 1910, 1914, 1915.

"How and Why Prohibition Came to America," 1920. A brief objective statement, translated in eleven countries.

THE NEW UNDERSTANDING MONOGRAPHS OF 1932-35

Is Liquor the Same Old Question?
Alcoholic Release and Expression
Alcoholic Pleasure: What Is It?
Should Social Drink Customs Be Accepted?
Alcoholic Culture: Should it be Retained?
Social Consequences of Alcoholic Drink
Alcoholic Pleasure and Public Safety
Alcoholic Release and Public Disorder
World Questioning of Alcoholic Pleasure
Alcoholic Personality
The Cult of Illusion
Alcoholic Expression and Personality

Selling Alcoholic Release
Outgrowing Alcoholic Culture
Slump and Resurgence in Liquor Culture

"Alcohol Trends in American College Life" (in the early Prohibition period).

"Drink in American Colleges" (before and after Prohibition period).

"Does Alcohol Aid Creative Ability?"

"Seeking A New Understanding," a study guide, for the Methodist Women's Society of Christian Service.

"A Modern Approach to the Problem of Alcohol." Three editions.

EDITOR

"Popularizing the Educational Approach to the Problems of Alcohol." Lectures at a Conference at Ohio State University, sponsored by the State Board of Education and the Intercollegiate Association.

"The International Student," 1915-1964; earlier, *"The Intercollegiate Statesman,"* 1902-1914; *"The Scientific Temperant Journal,"* 10 years, 1934-1943.

TABLE OF CONTENTS

SPIRIT OF 1900

"Account yourself happy if it be your lot to espouse some noble and unpopular cause in the beginning—to stand by its cradle, to help it grow, to see it first arouse curiosity, then attention, then contempt, then hatred, then fear, then respect, until at last over prejudice and hatred and party and old custom and vested interests, the irresistible current makes its way."

Senator Hoar of Massachusetts,
in a speech to Harvard students

This was the challenge that D. Leigh Colvin gave us, in 1900, the year we began to organize the Intercollegiate Prohibition Association.

PREFACE

IN VERY RECENT YEARS, the spirit of idealism that is so natural in most of us during our college years seems to express itself too often in destructive rebellion or irresponsible speech against almost anything—the college, the community, and even national and international affairs. It should be interesting, therefore, to study this particular problem, related as it is, though at opposite extremes, to idealism and irresponsible behavior.

The idealistic spirit that expressed itself in creative activities in the past is outstanding in the motivations and services of today's Peace Corps. At the beginning of the century this spirit was expressed in the student volunteers for Foreign Missions at the religious level, and in various civic movements at the secular level. The purpose of this book, however, is to express through the history of a different movement the service and spirit of idealism as shown in the evolution and growth of a movement which the author has shared with students, faculty, and alumni since 1900. Whatever the philosophy of such movements, whether temporary or permanent, radical or conservative, there is something vital shared by them all which, as in great experiments, leave a legacy of infinite value to the movements of today.

This book seeks to be objective, historically accurate, and factually based. It attempts to be realistic and conscious of the many directions in which educated youth may find themselves, especially in regard to convictions concerning social welfare and religious movements.

The form and style of the book, particularly the inclusion of story incidents with the historical matter, was strongly urged at the beginning of the project, in 1961, by students of Ohio State University who were working with me. They were Robert David Alkire, my editorial associate, and Elizabeth A. McCarthy and Patricia Jones, office secretaries. Later, at Otterbein College, I was assisted by Joan Hopkins, Becky Wiard, Lallie Yarman, and Mrs. Marjorie Corkery (wife of the Dean of Men). Thus, I was kept close to much of the student idealism and spirit of today.

One Saturday, at the close of office hours, while we were at twelve North Third Street, Columbus, Ohio, the cleaning woman entered the office and said:

"It's about time for you to go home."

"Well, yes and no," I answered. "I like my work here and want to stay as long as possible, and besides, I have no home—just a hotel room."

She replied, "I guess I have no home either. My husband drinks, it's terrible. I've done everything, I don't know what else to do, he gets mad at the very mention of A.A."

After saying a few of what I trust were helpful words, and the woman had departed, I dropped my head on the desk and said to myself: "Thank God for the privilege of being able to do something."

These days, even if it is at a very different level, such assistance is greatly needed and can be most far reaching. It might influence the basic educational approach to our present generation and might also help mould the future leaders of our culture and public opinion.

An Evolution in Understanding of the Problem of Alcohol

Chapter I

A HORSE, SLEIGHBELLS—AND THE BEGINNING*

ONE NEAR-ZERO NIGHT, in the horse and buggy years before the twentieth century, my brother Glenn and I were returning home with our parents after a church service in Wooster, Ohio. Huddled beneath a heavy blanket, we were well protected against the sharp west wind. Muffled as we were, we could hear the jingling bells of our one-horse sleigh and the familiar crunch of snow under the runners.

Suddenly old Tom stopped. Glenn and I poked our heads out and looked around curiously. There by the side of the road, in the middle of Killbuck Bottom, floundered two young fellows. They had obviously been having a night on the town in Wooster. One was drunk and insensible. His buddy, far better off, was trying to keep him awake and walking. Neither of them was an alcoholic or even an excessive drinker, they had just gone to town to "celebrate".

Father took us home and then went back to pick them up. He returned with them in the sleigh. That night Glenn and I heard one of them rolling the other around on the kitchen floor beneath our room, their grunts echoed audibly through the stovepipe. The next morning, when we came to breakfast, all traces of their visit were gone. This was my first encounter with the affects of alcohol. I remember vividly that one of those young fellows was near death; he was so intoxicated that he would have frozen in the zero degree weather if my father had not gone to his aid.

Sometime later, two younger brothers came across a neighbor who was flat on his face on the road at nearly the same location. Upon encountering the fellow, their horse stopped short—at least he had horse

* In order to make the book semi-autobiographical, the author here relates his background and how he became involved in the movements to solve the problems of alcoholism.

sense. Unfortunately, such incidents were frequent in the country. In towns and cities the police would pick up the drunks and give them shelter for the night. Such drunken behavior was certainly not good advertisement for business and culture.

One day at school an older boy arrived late. He took his seat, slouched across his desk, and then fell on the floor, much to the delight of the other students. Giggles and laughter filled the room, and it took the teacher several minutes to regain control.

Years later, a very different incident at the same school turned my attention to the field of service in which I have been engaged ever since. A magazine writer described the experience thusly:

> One early autumn night . . . a farmer boy of twelve or fourteen attended a schoolhouse prohibition meeting. There was a speaker of some ability whose name and message were soon forgotten, and there was a quartet of students from the college, Wooster, four miles away. The message of those students, rather the fact they were giving it, caught the young boy's imagination. Their rollicking, jolly good cheer and their personal service . . . placed a halo of idealism and respect around the undertaking they represented. That peppy team from Wooster College left an influence upon the life of Harry Warner greater than that of the speaker, effective though he may have been.[1]

Another incident in my boyhood years left a lasting impression. A well-known temperance speaker, Francis Murphy, a reformed drunkard and a great orator, came to Wooster for a two-week program on one of his pledge signing campaigns that took him throughout the United States. The entire town was excited. Large crowds attended, afternoon and night. My father took my brother and me. He signed the pledge himself, not because he needed to do so, but to share a sense of fellowship with those to whom this act meant a real change in life.

These crusades by reformed drunkards, "rehabilitated alcoholics" they would be called today, and other speakers and reformers, had been going on across the country for one hundred years, touching thousands of cities and towns, and reaching millions of people. Their common purpose was to reform alcoholics and promote total abstinence. Their chief method was the signing of abstinence pledges for life. Following emotional speeches that emphasized the poverty and degraded atmosphere of the drinker's family life, the drinkers were urged to sign these pledges.

1. "A Man in the Shadow", *National Magazine,* October, 1921.

Deeper than the memory of these incidents, however, was the quiet influence of my boyhood home and our Oak Chapel Church. I came to believe that alcoholic intoxication was a bad condition to be in and that liquor, because it made men drunk, could be seriously harmful to man and society. During my college years this belief was strengthened, and it grew into the conviction that the prevention of alcoholism would be a Christian service to school, community, and nation. During my years at Baldwin University I decided, once and for all, that I wanted to play a part in such a service.

At that time the saloon stood out as a serious threat to the general well-being of society. Practical citizens of our state had been trying for years to control the disorders of drunkenness, the fights that started within its swinging doors. In my mid-college years, when most students began to express the spirit of idealism and to take up some worthy cause in connection with it, the memories of the young fellows my father had rescued in Killbuck Bottom and of the boy who came to school drunk were not forgotten. My most interesting courses, history and sociology, raised certain questions. What could be done? My desire to do something about alcoholism grew. For my life's work I decided on social service rather than the ministry.

Toward the end of my junior year, the college YMCA selected two students, my friend Charles Mott and me, to attend a summer conference at Lake Geneva, Wisconsin. The ten days we spent there was a pivotal point in our lives. This was a period when the appeal of foreign mission service was very powerful. As many as 125 of the 600 students attending volunteered to give service in foreign lands. Many decided on careers in the ministry, a few went in for city settlement work, and still others chose YMCA work. No one, it seemed, thought of service to help reduce drinking and alcoholism. The need for men in this field was completely overlooked. But, although no one else volunteered to work in this area, I did.

In February, after graduation from Baldwin (now Baldwin-Wallace College), an opportunity suddenly opened. I received a letter from D. Leigh Colvin, a classmate of my brother at Ohio Wesleyan University. He asked me to join the Intercollegiate Prohibition Association, of which he was president, as his field secretary at $50.00 per month, with travel expenses to be raised enroute. Ten days later I was with Colvin in his room; I had one book on the problem of alcohol and a railroad guide. We spent Washington's Birthday mapping out a cross-country tour of colleges where we planned to organize study groups and public speaking contests. The following Monday morning, before daylight, I left for Otterbein College, where interest in our project was promising. By nightfall, a group of students had been organized into the first club in our new program. The next day I went to Denison, where a committee was formed. The third day, at Mount Union, resulted in another organization. The fourth day a beginning was made at Wooster, where I gave my first chapel talk. After a hearty reception at Baldwin where I had received my Ph.B. the previous June, I visited Heidelberg, Oberlin, Ohio Northern, DePauw (which had an active organization), Butler, Wabash, the University of Illinois, and five other colleges in Illinois; next I visited six colleges in Missouri, then went on to the University of Kansas. There, I met my first road-block in organizing. In spite of friendly support from faculty members, because of a mistake made by a student when handing in a chapel announcement for a group meeting, the president abruptly refused to permit any meeting and practically ordered me off the campus. Kansas was one of the three prohibition states at that time. After visiting State College in Manhattan, I was met by a very active group at Nebraska Wesleyan University of which Logan H. Roberts, at this time studying law in New York University, had been a member a year earlier. Then I continued through Iowa, Minnesota, and Wisconsin, reaching Chicago the last of May, where we set up our center of activities that autumn and remained for twenty-three years.

On my first day in Chicago, I called on Oliver W. Stewart, Chairman of the Prohibition Party, and found an opportunity for work in his office. The next day, I met Fred D. L. Squires, the student at the University of Chicago who had been writing a series of news stories about my tour for *The New Voice* of Chicago.[2] A young journalist who had devoted his life to the cause, he continued as one of the great newswriters, editors, and publicity men of the American anti-alcohol movement for fifty years. He has been one of my closest friends through the years since I met him in Snell Hall at the University that day in 1900.

It was in downtown Chicago in June, 1900, that the Intercollegiate Prohibition Association was reorganized and became stabilized. Previously, it had been an organization of undergraduates who met every

2. "The Opportunity of the Hour for College Men and Women", March, 1900.
"The Movement in the Colleges", March 25, 1900.
Report of Warner's Tour", April 12, 1900.
"A Personality Story (of Colvin)", April 12, 1900.
"Conferences for National Organization", July 13, 1900.

few years and carried on a series of oratorical contests and field activities in political campaign years. It now became an active, permanent association that soon began to focus major attention on educational purposes and programs. D. Leigh Colvin, Ohio Wesleyan, Delaware, Ohio, as last president of the former IPA, continued in the same position for sixteen of the next twenty years. *He was the founder* of the reorganization of 1900, and an effective organizer, speaker, and leader.

The National Oratorical Contest of 1900, held in a church in the center of the Chicago loop, drew a crowded and enthusiastic audience on one of the hottest nights of the summer. Colvin presided, I spent much of my time seeking ice water for the twelve students speaking from as many states. The winner was Rayner W. Kelsey, Earlham College, Richmond, Indiana; his subject, typical of this period in public speaking, was "Weighed in the Balance and Found Wanting".

The convention the next day included officers of the continuing IPA, students from the colleges that I had contacted on my organizing tour of three and a half months, state contest winners from twelve states, and students and professors who had caught the spirit of a new advance.

At the business meeting, Colvin was re-elected President; Virgil G. Hinshaw, Vice-President; Platte T. Amstutz, College of Wooster, a member of the Executive Committee; Edith Smith, Eureka College, Secretary; and Harry S. Warner, General Secretary and Treasurer.[3]

The conference of 1900 was held in close association with the national convention of the Prohibition Party that nominated John G. Woolley for President of the United States. It was the high-tide period of the Party and brought together an enthusiastic and aggressive attendence of delegates from every state. The students direct from the colleges and the rest of us in our IPA convention were stirred with enthusiasm by the dramatic incidents of the week. We began to dream and plan for a greatly enlarged intercollegiate movement that would reach all the colleges of the United States.

That summer and fall, Hinshaw went out as an advance-man for Oliver W. Stewart, Chairman of the Party, setting up whistle-stops and public rallies for the Presidential train that carried the candidates, John G. Woolley and Henry B. Metcalf, on a three months speaking campaign to election day in November. I had a place as secretary to the Chairman in the Chicago office; there was much to look after in his absence. One assignment was to bring out to the train, wherever it might

3. D. Leigh Colvin, *History of Prohibition,* pp. 323-326.

be, the most important letters and reports that came to the office. One day I joined the train early in the morning as it rolled east, then south from Lima, Ohio, to Columbus, in a continuous series of train-end meetings and town and city rallies. The meeting at Wooster, my hometown, was one of the most enthusiastic, but I took the chance to have a visit with my folks. Mother filled my travel bag with apples from the home orchard. Unfortunately, the official party beat us to the railway station. The train was gaining speed down the tracks. But, after furious waving, it came back—that was once, at least, when a Presidential Special Train backed up a half mile to pick up a left-behind!

Continuing Organization of Student Groups

In frequent conferences that summer to plan for a permanent organization and the program for the first year, Colvin, Hinshaw and I decided to reach more colleges, form more clubs for study and oratorical contests, set up state organizations, and let the Association grow out of experience with the cooperation of the increasing number of students thus enlisted in the movement.[4] We adopted one policy that became the basis of our continuity through the years—to visit and re-visit each local group every year.

Beginning in September, President Colvin made his first organizing tour in Kentucky, Pennsylvania, Connecticut, and New Jersey. He organized almost "every institution visited", eighteen in Pennsylvania alone. Virgil Hinshaw, after completing his job of organizing local committees to arrange the itinerary of the Woolley Presidential Train through New York state, discontinued his political work and organized seven IPA clubs in the colleges of New York. I revisited the clubs I had organized earlier in Wisconsin and Indiana. There were about 100 local college groups by the end of 1900.

We had no office, each of us did his own correspondence and raised most of the money he received on salary and travel expenses. With the beginning of 1901, I rented a typewriter, learned the "hunt and pick" method, rented a mimeograph, and used my $10.00 a month room on Oakwood Boulevard, Chicago, as our office. Leigh and Virgil took to the college trail and continued traveling much of the time for more than fifteen years thereafter. I became headquarters secretary and writer of study programs.

After New Year's, 1901, Colvin and I re-visited the college groups

4. *Standard Encyclopedia of the Alcohol Problem,* vol. III, p. 1327.

that we had organized the previous year. Shortly thereafter, I entered the University of Chicago for graduate study in sociology and Colvin, following a tour of the northwestern colleges, entered the University of California for work in political science.

At Chicago I found a group that Fred Squires had formed the previous June before graduating. We set up a course of lectures, including faculty members, temperance leaders, and John G. Woolley, Prohibition candidate for President of the United States the previous year. Woolley had been a successful lawyer and civic leader in Minneapolis—and a heavy drinker. Changed by religious experience, he partially overcame his bout with alcohol and gave his life to the Cause. A great orator, he handled the English language in such a way that a university professor classified him among the greatest masters of English in America. Woolley fought drunkenness to save himself as well as others; but he was always an alcoholic. Once or twice a year, he would disappear into some hotel on a "binge" and fight it out alone. He died in a hotel in Spain from alcoholism, while on a speaking tour through Europe for the World League Against Alcoholism.

CHAPTER II

CHALLENGE OF THE FIRST DECADE

THE SPIRIT OF THE COLLEGE IDEALISTS, in 1900, who began to share in the American movement to reduce and ultimately remove the burdens of alcoholic drink and alcoholism, was one of quick response to what they saw as perhaps the greatest welfare problem of their age. They wanted to do something about it. It was much the same as the spirit of similar-minded college students and graduates of recent years who have seen the world-wide vision of the Peace Corps, which seeks to counteract the ideology and propaganda of Communism by having individuals take part personally at points where service can be directly helpful.

Such fields offer today—and always will offer—visions of public service to which aspiring graduates may give a few adventurous years, gain experience, and perhaps devote a life.

This spirit of idealism, which is normal in many of us in our college years, found an outlet and opportunity for expression in the growing movements against alcoholic drink from 1900 onward. Led by deeply concerned but very realistic young men and women, it grew strong and became a working force in colleges for thirty years. Thus, the desire to have a part in the practical job of seeking to "drive out the saloon" or to reduce the area of drink-selling by local option or state prohibition became a natural field in which to test idealism—an exciting adventure and a very practical service.

The desire gradually became more popular, as in other welfare reforms, religious, and patriotic movements at other periods. An outstanding example was the Student Volunteer Movement for Foreign Missions which, for a half-century, encouraged students to study the religious cultures of other countries and to enlist for foreign service. One of their slogans, "To make friends for America around the World," has become a rallying call of the Peace Corps, that works today in South America, Africa, and East Asiatic countries.

The Vision of 1900

To the re-organizers of the Intercollegiate Prohibition Association of 1900, this appeal brought a sense of concern, responsibility, and dedication that led most of them to give life-time service to reduce and, hopefully, to eliminate alcoholic drunkenness from everyday living. Three of the first five accepted, lived the life challenge; three or more of the next five did the same. Many others during the following creative years gave part or full-time and usually sacrificial service. They shared directly as secretaries in the Association or continued as lay-workers. Other thousands of those who studied the problem while in college became leaders in the educational, promotional, scientific, and political activities of America at the local, state, national, and international levels during the half-century that followed.

The First Five Years

Seeking from its first year to form a lasting organization in the colleges of the country, the IPA began to grow steadily in the number of local groups organized. Gradually it became recognized as a student movement of the period. With two to five secretaries traveling from college to college, reports began to arrive in a steady stream by the middle of the second year. The clubs that had been active previous to 1900, Kalamazoo, Ohio Wesleyan, Cornell University, Nebraska Wesleyan, DePauw, and others, added educational programs to their public speaking contests.

Within two years after 1900, as Leigh, Virgil and I began to get our oratorical contest and local-study program under way, five very recent graduates came into the Association as founding members and field secretaries: Alfred C. Millican, University of Washington; Platte T. Amstutz, College of Wooster; Herbert C. Shattuck, Cornell University; Logan H. Roberts, Nebraska Wesleyan; and Daniel A. Poling, Dallas College, Oregon, at age nineteen, the youngest of us all.

While in our college years all of us had become concerned about alcoholic drink, drunkenness and the centers from which the culture of intoxication—the saloons, the taverns—flowed out into the communities in which we lived. We wanted to do something about it.

D. Leigh Colvin, raised in the culture of crusading abstainers, gave credit for his conviction to his mother who "instilled in me an undying hatred of the drink traffic" as she had seen it before her early death which left him an orphan. A boy from the farm, I had seen drunkenness among schoolmates and in the pinched living of farm homes when farmers, taking the farm produce to market, returned toxic-happy, but with few groceries for their families. I had also seen what a quartet of Wooster College students, with a speaker in a country schoolhouse meeting, could do to change youthful attitudes about the saloon.

Later, on my first tour among colleges, I found seven other students who wanted to give similar service. Four of them did. Among these was Virgil G. Hinshaw, Penn College, Iowa, who at once started a club, entered the oratorical contests of the IPA, came to the organizing conference in Chicago and was elected Vice-President.

In 1902, President Colvin, on his first tour in the Northwest, found interest already active among both students and instructors of the area, as a result of previous work done by Alfred C. Millican and Daniel A. Poling. While students they had organized clubs widely in the colleges of this area.

The University of Washington study group was examining the customs and cultural sides of the alcohol problem, insisting that all aspects, pro and con, should be better known. At Oregon State College, Corvallis, the League became the largest on the Pacific Coast as women students joined in normal proportion. Coed cooperation was rare in other parts of the country. At Eugene Divinity School the group was seeking effective ways to reach the public and find methods of solution.

Two new field secretaries came into service that year (1902) at the national level—Daniel A. Poling and Logan H. Roberts—Roberts with both law and masters degrees. Both came from deeply Christian homes. Dan was the son of a college president. He had experienced the realism of rowdy men coming to town from the Oregon lumber camps to get drunk and to find a sense of release after months of seclusion in the logging camps of the state.

Logan had been active as a student in a club at Nebraska Wesleyan University. He planned to give a substantial part of his life to the Cause. His field as traveling secretary was Iowa, Nebraska, Kansas, and Colorado. While in Kansas, he found what he called a "revelation".

> My entrance into the prohibition state of Kansas was a revelation of the efficiency and rightness of the principle for which we are working—prohibition is first, last, and always a success. Comparing these towns with places of the same size in the saloon states, I talked with many in stores, banks, hotels, and on the street. Not a single one favored the open

> saloon. Bank deposits were safer as was the credit business. Poverty was almost unknown, colleges crowded, and students almost unanimous in support of the "dry" law.

Logan Roberts, as traveling secretary in the Central-Western states, stirred student enthusiasm and picked up expense money wherever he went, including the first $500 contribution the Association had yet received. On leaving, he assured us that he would provide substantial support later. This he did years after by creating a trust fund with an annual income, because, as he said to me, "You stuck to it!"

In 1901, Charles M. Hay, Central College, Fayette, Missouri, won highest national honors in an IPA oratorical contest at Buffalo, New York, made up of prohibition leaders and visitors at the Pan American World Exposition of that year. Hay became a secretary of the IPA and a lifetime worker for the Anti-Saloon League. He was repeatedly elected to the state legislature and was a United States Senator at the time that the National Movement adopted he Eighteenth Amendment, fifteen years after he began as a student.

In 1904, the Association began to encourage devotion to the Cause by circulating the following pledge:

> Whether engaged in a regular profession, business or occupation or giving my whole time to the larger fulfillment of the pledge, I will find for myself an active field of labor in the cause.

The public occasion for taking this determined stand was stated in an editorial in the *Intercollegiate Statesman,* May 15, 1906:

> In governmental affairs, a new social conscience is recognizing the reformer type of statesman. He is given credit and honor instead of being criticized as a visionary and a busy-body. People honor without intermediate machinery or party tag the manhood of Folk, Roosevelt, La Follette, Bryan, Hanley, Berry, and Castle, and what they have done against boss rule and against corporate control.

Under the steady leadership of such dedicated young idealists just out of college, and of a continuous accession of others year by year thereafter, our program of visiting colleges each year continued until it was cut short seventeen years after it began, as the United States entered World War I. Through all these years, it was the policy of the Association, in its direct contacts with college students, to keep young men, recent graduates, at the front.

Successive Groups of Volunteers

After the first years, many recent college graduates, who had been gaining experience in the local colleges, came into the field service of the Association. They were Hervey F. Smith, Baker University, Kansas; Samuel F. Grathwell, Berea College, Kentucky; Elon G. Borton, Greenville College, Illinois; Harley H. Gill, Morningside College, Iowa; and J. Raymond Schmidt, DePauw University, Greencastle, Indiana.

For thirteen years Elon G. Borton devoted himself to executive service and the promotion of study. On his first visit to Berea College, he discovered Sam Grathwell who had worked his way out of the slums of Cincinnati. Sam's father had died an alcoholic. Hervey F. Smith came into the movement from a very different background, a Christian home in a prohibition state, where as a youth he had seen nothing of what it meant to have a saloon in the community.

Harley H. Gill came from an orphanage in Iowa. A neighbor boy had been helping his mother raise cucumbers and getting them to town, then detouring home with the check to keep his father from grabbing it for liquor. The vivid experience that Harley gained from this family gave him a reaction against drunkenness. It led him at age eighteen, while attending a preparatory school and Morningside College, to begin work for the State Prohibition Committee of Minnesota.

In a personal letter, sixty years later, Harley Gill described that memorable childhood experience:

> The strain on the mother became too great; she was sent to a state insane asylum. During the months that she was there, the father got hold of himself and did not touch a drop. The mother improved and she was permitted to return home, just before Christmas; what a happy family that was! The father, on an errand downtown, fell in with a bunch of old-time cronies who almost dragged him into a saloon for "just one drink" to celebrate Christmas and his wife's return. He went home crazy drunk. The next morning, the broken body of the wife and mother was found on a railroad track a mile away. The word spread among the children of our orphanage. Christmas was a terrible day for us.

Campus Drinking

In general, the Association gave its attention mainly to the public problems of alcohol—the social, political, and economic sources and consequences. Drinking and drink customs were incidental to its education program; they were the concern of the college, the student councils, and the discipline officers. The Association had no sympathy at all with drink-traditions, nor did it do much about them. It encouraged objective study as the necessary base *for intelligent, personal, and group decision and action.*

Through study, discussion, and participation in outside programs of action, students were encouraged to look at the drink problem as a whole to see its seriousness and to become personally concerned.

Yet the activities of the local groups often grew into positive action on the campus. Through objective study and discussion, they came to look at the subject honestly. They became concerned. Out of this concern, there developed sometimes direct campus action in support of restrictive regulations and campaigns against drink tradition.

The Case of Harry Platz

An illustration of what a group and a strong individual could do occurred at the University of California. The club was organized as a study group by Leigh Colvin in 1904. It prospered in its activities for six years. Then it took a stand against certain practices that were disgracing University traditions. One was the drunkenness that followed the annual tussle around the "Big C" at the top of the hill, between Stanford and California, at midnight preceding the final football game of the season. As reported at the time:

> "Beer night" around the "Big C" on the hillside of the University of California is a thing of the past, thanks to Harry Platz of the Intercollegiate Prohibition Association. Up until 1910, a good deal of drinking took place around the "Big C," an immense letter built into the mountain side in 1902 in solid concrete two feet deep. It is the duty and honor of the sophomore class to protect it from rival university depredations on the nights preceding the big games with Stanford. The class furnished a force of men to guard the monument all night lest the opposition succeed in their attempts to "paint it red." It had been the tradition that the fellows could not remain awake without "booze." The beer was delivered in kegs in spite of the fact that this is a part of the campus, and a state law forbids the sale of liquor within one mile of the state university grounds.
>
> When it came the turn of the class of Harry Platz to guard the "Big C," Platz tried to have the beer excluded. He was supported by a strong element in the city who offered to furnish, free, all the sandwiches, doughnuts, and coffee needed; it was decided to have no beer. However, toward midnight, the beer kegs began to come up the hill. Many who did not

drink went home, but Platz and a chum or two remained through the night. The next day, they took up the legal end of the matter with the prosecuting attorney. The faculty lent support, and the sentiment in the class grew stronger, and the midnight carousals around the university's emblem on the hillside came to an end. An authority of the university congratulated Platz heartily on his victory and quietly warned him against becoming a martyr.

The next year, Platz led a battle to amend the constitution of the student body, forbidding the drinking of intoxicants at any function of the university. The petition was killed, but the resolution put on record the student sentiment against liquor by a vote of 627 to 138.

Practical Idealism—Then and Now

The spirit of the realistic-idealists who shared in the movement through these years as students has been one of quick response and devotion to a great national need. It was much the same, if not wholly so, as the spirit and vision of the National Peace Corps today, which seeks to counteract the ideology and results of Communism by taking personal part at critical points where most needed. Both offered visions of public service to which students might give a few adventurous years, gain experience, or, perhaps, devote a lifetime. But, there were these differences: The IPA volunteers of a half-century ago began without training and had very little money for support.

To the organizers, the appeal did become a lifetime job—a full-time dedication of service toward the reduction and ultimate elimination of alcoholic drunkenness from everyday living. Three of the first five accepted and lived the full-time life challenge; three or more of the next five did the same. Many others during the following creative years gave time, service, and sacrifice as field secretaries in the Association or continued as lay-workers. Thousands of those who studied the problem under the initiative of the Association while in college became leaders in the educational, promotional, scientific, and political activities at local, state, national, and international levels during the half-century that followed.

CHAPTER III

INITIATING STUDY OF THE PROBLEM

THE COMMISSION GIVEN ME by D. Leigh Colvin, President of the Association, then in his senior year at Ohio Wesleyan, as I left his student room that February day in 1900 before daylight for our first organizing tour of three and a half months among the colleges of nine central-western states was:

There should be a thorough study of all sides of the problem.
Every interest of society should be taken into consideration.

Thus, from the very first year the organizers and secretaries of the Association, as students just a year or two out of college, began to be interested in obtaining and promoting a more objective understanding of *The Problem* than was being expressed in the emotional appeals and writings of many outstanding temperance movement leaders of that period.

The Days of the Typical Saloon

This was the period of the typical saloon. Liquor was available and inexpensive to all who sought it, except in three states and in many small communities. Saloons in Chicago and other cities advertised free lunch standing ready on the bar. Large cities, small towns, and country cross-roads had drinking places. In the foreign colonies of the big cities, beer was delivered to the home; "high society" used various imported wines; Kentucky whiskies were popular; cider was intentionally turned hard in farmers' cellars; "moonshine" flourished in the southern mountains and bootleggers were as rampant then as later in prohibition years. The saloon was the place where men went to drink, remained to boast and receive the news, and shout "set it up" and drink again. In factory areas, the saloon was the poor man's club. Elsewhere it was the profligates' club for the sons of the well-to-do.

In this general situation, the main program of those who were leading the anti-alcohol movement was directed toward removing the legal saloon as the place of too easy and too abundant access to the intoxicating "poison". Friends of the drink customs did not try to defend the ordinary saloon, much less the disreputable ones. Frequently during these years, salesmen for the industry complained that many selling places were a headache to the trade. Occasionally, organizations were formed to make it respectable, a social club for the community. From the opposite direction a feeling was growing among the leaders of the temperance and abstinence movements. This feeling became the conviction that the only measures adequate were those that legally tended to reduce both the production and sale of liquor.

The Problem as Understood

By 1900, the alcohol problem was generally understood by those seeking a solution to be the "liquor traffic" in its political and economic aspects, the saloon and drunkenness. One main reason for the determined, enthusiastic, and perhaps radical attitudes among these concerned was the conviction that the industry was making excessive profits out of its influence in public affairs, and this included the illegal as well as legal promotion of its products. It was readily acknowledged that there were many serious social questions related to drink that were not alone due to alcohol: such as a much degraded family life and juvenile delinquency. But these questions, it was felt, could be solved only, or better, after the liquor traffic had been curbed or destroyed. "Drink" was regarded as so active and deteriorating a factor that it would handicap, if not defeat, many other efforts toward social reform.

Beginnings of Objective Study

The Intercollegiate Association undertook a different approach to the "drinking problem" than that of other agencies of the period. It began to center attention on many important aspects as necessary both to personal decision and to individual or group action. It did not discount the value of educational propaganda, indeed, it often shared in it. But it did encourage action, especially after a decision had been made intelligently and for reasons of value. The Association did not then, or ever afterward, promote a total abstinence pledge. Frequently, students from drinking homes, including sons of saloon keepers, joined the local clubs to study the question. Once the son of a wealthy brewer in Minneapolis, active in the league at the university, aided in research and came out against the drink customs of his family. The fact that he later yielded to the pressure of his family inheritance was not a blot on the sincerity of his attitude while a student. It was just an ordinary instance of family pressure.

From the beginning the Intercollegiate Association took the position that objective study should be the basis for personal decision of whether to drink or not to drink, and as the basis for social action. It was agreed that this study should include a range of factual knowledge. Thus, our main program of these years was to organize study classes, discussion groups, and oratorical contests as incentives to study.

Students Desire to Know All Sides

The experience gained in our first two years in setting up these groups brought to light a very real desire among college students to have a deeper understanding than they had previously gained from schools, churches, and family relationships. There were few books available and no study plans or outlines. No related courses of instruction were then being offered by the colleges. Those who were trying to solve this gigantic social problem were doing it by realistic, emotional reaction and practical observation, but with little scientific knowledge.

Therefore, even within the first year, we began to prepare study material that we hoped would be more helpful as a beginning for our study groups. The first was a one-sheet outline that gave the basic elements concerning the question of alcoholic drink, as understood at that time. By the third year, we were publishing a periodical to distribute these studies, and our traveling secretaries were visiting and promoting their use in one hundred or more colleges each year. This was the origin of *The Intercollegiate Statesman* that continued this program through 1918. In 1924, this magazine was renamed *The International Student*. At that time we had correspondents in twenty-three countries.

When we began to create this new study material, in 1901, the political aspects of the alcohol problem were outstanding. Generally, efforts to improve the situation were centered in the philosophies back of local option, state prohibition, and related activities that tended toward governmental action. Most of the leaders in the various organizations were convinced that the system of licensing the sale of alcoholic beverages was both immoral and illegal. The more aggressive opponents were saying that it "could never be licensed without sin!" Some legal authorities questioned the policy of license as insufficient control over the sale of intoxicants. High court decision supported the philosophy that "License gives legal standing which it does not otherwise have." Crowley versus Christenson, U.S. 86, 1890 stated:

> By the general concensus of opinion of every civilized and Christian community, there are very few sources of crime and misery to society equal to the dram shop, where intoxicating liquor in small quantities, to be drunk at the time, are sold indiscriminately to all parties that apply . . . . The police power of the state is fully competent to regulate the business, to mitigate its evils, or to suppress it entirely.

The first studies that the Association prepared were to learn just what rights the saloon had under constitutional law. If this could rightly be understood, it was believed that one serious roadblock to reform could be removed and that social and educational forces could then act freely; that the burden of drunkenness could be reduced and gradually eliminated; and that education by public schools, churches, group discussions, and similar activities would be able to bring about reform in the normal ways of social progress.

These studies, planned and revised at frequent conferences of the secretaries, were written by myself and published in the magazine of the Association. They were followed by a series of studies that reflected successive steps in understanding at later periods.

Out of this understanding came the first series of sixteen studies, *The Political Phases of Prohibition,* with such subdivisions as: "The Liquor Traffic, A Political Problem", "Rights of the Seller", "Public Safety and Liquor Laws", "Property Rights", "The Principle of License", "Public Control: The Gothenberg Method of Sweden", "State Monopoly and the Liquor Traffic", "Local Option", "State Prohibition", "Legal and Moral Results", and others.

This series was followed by *The Social Aspects* that included sixteen main topics, such as: "The Drink Habit—A Social Problem", "Alcohol and Public Health", "The Public Cost", "Industrial Welfare", "The Question of Crime", "The Traffic and Law", "The Traffic in Politics", "The Traffic and the Church", "The Educational Force of Law", and "The Sphere for Government".

The third series centered attention on a wider understanding of the problem to aid solution. The following are the titles of the studies of the succeeding six years: "Government and the Liquor Traffic", "Social Welfare and the Alcohol Problem", "The Relation of Liquor to Other Social Problems", "The Social Demands for Prohibition", and "A Comparison of Methods".

Growing into an Inter-Campus School

The study-group program that we had started our first year in local clubs spread so widely and had improved so greatly in content that it came to be called, by President Colvin fifteen years later, "One vast training school for developing leaders and workers."

In fact, it was just such a training school. One year, 125 college teachers enrolled 2,500 students in classes in these studies. Thus, 2,500 students were receiving systematic instruction that year on the problem.

It was a unique and efficient school—a school without a dollar of endowment—one that did college level work without the cost of buildings or instruction. It accomplished a program of education by utilizing the assistance of interested professors and the use of classrooms wherever it was accepted. The traveling secretaries encouraged the desire for systematic instruction, helped organize the classes, and assisted in procuring the instructors. Colvin and myself were both authors of courses of instruction and books relating to the problem.

Dr. Colvin handled the economics and political science phases and I was in charge of the sociological aspects. My *Social Welfare and the Liquor Problem* was being used more than any other book of those years for study of the problem, both in and outside of colleges. It was chosen as the most useful book for that purpose in America in a survey made by a Presbyterian Church Board. More and more colleges began to include class instruction or a series of lectures at the request of students. In very few instances would these courses have been offered had it not been for the interest aroused by the field secretaries of the Association.

Gradually, instruction began to be offered as a credit course in such institutions as: the University of California, Nebraska Wesleyan, the University of Southern California, Albion College, Cornell College, Iowa Wesleyan, Simpson, Georgetown, Macalester, Carleton, Muskingum, the University of Florida, and Washington State College. These were the earliest, and others followed.

Lecture Courses

The courses offered in 1913-14 by universities, usually by professors of the highest standing in their departments, were such as the following:

> The University of Wisconsin, eight lectures; "The Industrial Aspects of the Liquor Problem", "The Traffic in Politics and Government", "The Legal Ethics of the Saloon", "Sources of the Liquor Institution", "Social

Aspects of the Liquor Problem", and "Alcohol and Health".

Cornell University, six lectures: "The Place of Law in the Control of the Liquor Traffic", "Alcohol as a Factor in Evolution", "Why People Stupefy Themselves", "The New York Legislature and Liquor Politics", "Prohibition as a Solution for Our Industrial Problems", and "The Evolution of the Anti-Liquor Movement".

The University of Minnesota: "Alcohol and Health", "Philosophy of Prohibition". "Liquor and Morals", and "Liquor and Immigration".

By 1916, Syracuse University had a study series covering: "Social Aspects of the Liquor Problem", "Alcohol and the Demands of Efficiency", "The Evolution of Public Sentiment", and "Prospects for National Prohibition".

DePauw University had a series on "The Chemistry of Alcohol", and "Alcohol and Politics in Indiana".

Ohio Wesleyan University: "Historical Development of the Temperance Movement", "The Liquor Problem from the Businessman's Viewpoint", "Physical Effects of Alcohol", "The Psychology of Intemperance", "The Economic Phase of the Problem", and "Legal Aspects of the Liquor Problem".

The next year, 1914-15, President Colvin gave lectures on the political science, economic, and historical aspects at Princeton, Harvard, Yale, Brown, Dartmouth, Boston School of Theology, Hartford Theological School, Wesleyan, Minnesota, Ohio State, Pennsylvania State College, and others.

Following the spread of such substantial educational activities on the Alcohol Problem and the increasing attention given to it in curriculum instruction, the Intercollegiate Association discontinued its direct activities in this field. Twenty years later, under the vastly different public conditions and attitudes that followed the repeal of the prohibition movement, it began to encourage the use of special lecturers, who could discuss the problems relating to alcohol in a fully objective and scientific approach that would take into account the latest results of research and experience. Such lecturing was done by Dr. Albion Roy King, professor of Philosophy at Cornell University, who gave particular attention to "The Psycholology of Alcoholism" and "Basic Information". In this approach, Dr. King became an outstanding leader.

CHAPTER IV

GROWING UNDERSTANDING LEADS TO GREATER OPPORTUNITIES

AT THE BEGINNING OF OUR SECOND DECADE of activity, in 1910, "the college movement" as represented by the Intercollegiate Prohibition Association had gained a place of greater influence outside its own field than even we recognized at the time. We were too close to it.

We had already interested and trained, to a substantial degree, many students of two and a half college generations. Our educational program had gained a place among extra-curricular activities and had begun to encourage professors to offer credit courses of instruction. Also, the field experiences of student groups in off-campus campaigns had caught the attention of the various organizations that were engaged in the local option, state and national anti-alcohol movements of that period. Many recent graduates had already become active leaders. But some of them were concerned about the divergent philosophies or ideologies and the lack of unity in the larger organizations, particularly the Prohibition Party and the Anti-Saloon League. The latter, by this time, had become the outstanding leader of the general movement.

Back in 1873, the Prohibition Party, following a pattern set by the Republican Party in its relation to slavery, took the position that a great reform must have the support of a political party to carry it through and insure continued enforcement. The League organized much later under different national circumstances took the position that the reform could be brought about by many nonpartisian steps such as strict legal control, refusal to grant license to sell, local option, and state prohibition. Possibly later it could be reformed at the national level.

The rivalry between these ideologies came to be an embarrassment in our work in the colleges. It was often a hot subject of discussion but it did not seem necessary to many of our IPA alumni who had become active in either one or both of these major stratagies. This divergence in philosophy was highly controversial at the time the IPA launched its first all-college convention in 1910.

The Valparaiso Convention

By June, 1910, the date of the convention at Valparaiso University, Valparaiso, Indiana, nine states had enacted prohibition—Alabama, Georgia, Kansas, Maine, Mississippi, North Carolina, North Dakota, Oklahoma, and Tennessee. The Legislatures of four other states that did not have some form of prohibition or local veto, passed local option laws. This left only five states and three territories without some form of local veto. It is estimated that 41,000,000 people were living in "dry" territory.

This was the year that the consumption of intoxicating beverages, measured by absolute alcohol content, reached its highest peak, or the plateau on which it remained stationary for four years before it began to recede.

The call for the convention gave the following objectives:

1. To impress upon educated men their duty to prepare for the adult responsibility of entering into public political service.
2. To give students a vision of the opportunity that would come from having a part in the banishment of liquor.
3. To encourage students to concentrate upon this major issue so that their opportunity would not be lost in questions of method, or of which organization would be leader in the battle at the national level.

Virgil G. Hinshaw, Association President at this time, made an appeal in his opening address for greater unity as an outstanding need among the non-alcohol movements. He showed how the younger men who had studied the problem together as students could bring harmony in spirit and program, if not in the philosophies of the organizations that were striving for leadership—the National Anti-Saloon League and the Prohibition Party. He stated as follows:

> Whatever are the merits of the positions taken by these two great contending organizations, this convention is not the battle ground . . . (it) is for the purpose of studying the various methods of attack against the liquor traffic . . . . We are taking into account the work of many agencies that should work together . . . where specialists may meet to teach and compare methods. Let there be the utmost freedom of discussion.

To this he added:

> . . . even in this period of controversy, the Association should carry on

its educating policy applying it to train thinkers and leaders . . . . In this capacity it reaches more than 50,000 students each year and inspires hundreds to engage actively in some phase of reform activity.

On the program of this first separate and national college student convention there were speakers from both the League and the Party. The students attending included supporters of both ideologies—the majority being in between or undecided. It was one of the first conventions at the national level at which speakers from both ideologies appeared on the same platform.

In his address on "College Men in the Anti-Liquor Crusade", E. S. Shumaker, Superintendent of the Anti-Saloon League of Indiana, reported that students and faculty members had contributed greatly to the county option campaigns of two previous years in the Hoosier state. He was so impressed by this service that he had asked the colleges of Indiana to prepare courses of systematic instruction on the problem.

Oliver W. Stewart, Chairman of the Prohibition Party, won support for the principles of the party by the keen logic with which he presented historical background and the meaning and ideals of that approach.

The addresses by secretaries of the Association included: "The Working of the Local League" and "Enlisting Students in Large Universities" by Harley H. Gill and Hervey F. Smith. As General Secretary, I reported in detail the activities and rapid growth of the Association.

In a call for state reports of work being done, those by Brown of Illinois, Schmidt of Indiana, Barrett of Iowa, Nelson of Kansas, Loveless of Florida, Short of Pennsylvania, and Coon of South Dakota brought out facts, statistics, stories, and accomplishments by students during the previous year that were beyond all reasonable expectations.

On Sunday, the closing day, Dr. Samuel Dickie, President of Albion College, gave an objective analysis of the national situation. Two inspirational addresses by our youthful Vice-President, Daniel A. Poling, and one by Oliver W. Stewart, were strong appeals for service from the background of their own college-enlisted devotion to the cause. Dan related how he had joined the Association at nineteen, when Colvin visited Dallas College in Oregon, during his first tour among Pacific coast colleges.

Fifty-Three on the Hillside

Early Sunday morning, fifty-three delegates from nearly as many states met in a devotional service above the reflecting water of Sager's Lake.

Then, as always, the water seemed to mirror the deep sincerity of college ideals. In the shade of the trees by the lake, the group shared in a quiet study of the spiritual conviction that prompted them to give service as Christian citizens to the movement against the social consequences of alcoholic drink. Many in the group that morning, as I recall, did give from half to full lifetime service to the cause in the years that followed.

We talked about the teachings of Jesus that seemed to apply directly to college trained young men when seeking the spiritual meaning of life in public affairs, particularly in hard jobs such as those we were facing at this convention. The following is an extract from the talk, "A Message to the Strong", which I gave that morning:

> That higher education means greater responsibility for service to humanity we are beginning to acknowledge. Note the growing number entering social settlement and similar services, either by giving themselves or by enabling others to do so. Yet, we miss the application of educated capacity to the place where it means dealing with the masses of humanity in the most authoritative of all capacities—government and political reform.
>
> We leave government to the bribe-takers and public opinion to the bribe-givers. Reform is related to "cranks", extremists, and the ignorant-if-devoted. The saloon is a necessary social tool of the corrupt politican. By controlling the central wards of our great cities, it tends to fix the public ideals of the nation far below the point where free play of the democratic process indicates they should be.
>
> That field of service which Edmund Burk said requires the greatest capacity of which the human mind is capable—the government of ourselves and our fellows—politics—we leave to the worn out agglomeration of sentiments, called parties, the liquor controlling "bosses", the "interests" of which whisky is the vilest, yet the most publicly sanctionized. Government is left too much to "politics for profit", not for service.
>
> No more vital motive lies before the conscientious college man today than to enter politics for service, reform for principle. The very scarcity of high thinking men who seek this field is a call for those who have the vision to come right, to serve the country in the anti-liquor movement, and in the political reforms that must go with it. It is, therefore, a serious duty of college men to prepare to have an active part in reform politics, to put an end to the Tammanys, the Hinky Dinks, The Quays, and the saloon gang of voters and vote makers. No one can overestimate the blight of such leadership or estimate too highly the strengthening that comes to our morale and the morals of our national life when well trained young men face the responsibilities of reform seriously.

Major Steps Toward Cooperation

Following this first independent convention of the Association, the philosophy and field service of the IPA grew increasingly cooperative with all the anti-alcohol movements of the day, particularly the Anti-Saloon League. Most of the members of the college groups were now interested in the practical program of the League and in having a part in the thousands of local option, state-wide and anti-license campaigns then going on to refuse to license or to vote out saloons. "To study" was not enough. To have a hand in field activities was more exciting. More groups had already taken part in surveys of community attitudes, saloon surroundings, apprehension of violators of the law, and in speaking and providing music for public meetings.

The advantage of holding our top-level oratorical contests at the great conventions of the League always gave us large attendance, an enthusiastic crowd, and gained public support and publicity as a first night attraction. These were realistic factors.

College Idealism in the Anti-Saloon League Movement

During the first years after 1900, there had come into the Anti-Saloon League, then the largest anti-alcohol movement in America, a group of young men directly out of college. They had been inspired by the meaning of this new non-partisan movement and by the personal leadership of Howard H. Russell, who founded the Anti-Saloon League at Oberlin College in 1893. Russell was an idealist, an inspiring orator, and a young man of extraordinary vision and personal drive. A graduate of Oberlin College of Theology, he had caught the vision of service in the swelling reaction of the period against the drunkenness that had continued to increase during the century. As a young man with a vision, he had given five years to the ministry, mostly at the Armour Mission which was associated with the Armour Institute on the edge of the Chicago slum area. Here, the overwhelming evidence of how people lived in a liquor soaked section of a great city so appalled him that he decided to give himself in life service to the Cause. He returned to Oberlin, called together a few leaders, and organized the Ohio Anti-Saloon League.

Among his first associates, he enlisted students and recent graduates to join him in ASL service. Two of these, in addition to himself, gave their lives fully to the Cause, as state, national, and world leaders in the great Anti-Saloon League movement of the century. They were: Wayne B. Wheeler, Oberlin College, who spent his years in the legal department; and Ernest H. Cherrington, Ohio Wesleyan, who became the Educational Director of the League and publisher of the greatest volume of temperance promotional material ever issued from one source and, after 1920, founder of the World League Against Alcoholism.

Cherrington came into the Anti-Saloon League as a dedicated student. The Anti-Saloon League of America had just gained a place of recognized leadership, and he saw in the movement the challenge of service to a great cause. He at once took part in local campaigns. In 1902, he became a district Superintendent in Ohio. After two years there, he was sent to be Superintendent of the League in the state of Washington. When the League began publishing *The American Issue* in Chicago, he became associate editor. When the League set up a National publishing house, in Westerville, Ohio, he became editor and manager of publications. Through the years, *The American Issue* was published in as many as thirty-five editions. For many years Dr. Cherrington continued to be head of the educational department of the League, until it was reorganized under his leadership as "The Temperance Education Foundation".

In the second decade, 1910 and after, many students in widely scattered colleges throughout the country gave service through the IPA clubs in their colleges. At Otterbein, Edward H. Dailey, who was earning his way through college in the publishing department of the National Anti-Saloon League, was an active member all through his college years. Later, he traveled widely throughout the country lecturing and setting up community and church meetings. After a period of highly successful service to the ministry, he returned to the Cause at the most critical point of the mid-century and became Executive Secretary of the Temperance Education Foundation and successor to Dr. Cherrington.

Vernon L. Phillips was very active in the same group at Otterbein at about the same period. He became a field secretary and a national officer of the Intercollegiate Association and gave the major part of his first years after graduation to service in three or four of the national activities of the period. After the Armistice, November 11, 1918, that ended World War I, he gave two years in raising funds to aid in educational and recreational programs among the American soldiers in France, many of whom had to wait two years for transportation home.

In 1910, Braxton B. Wade, a student at Texas Christian University, attended the Intercollegiate Convention at Valparaiso. He had previously caught the attention of the Librarian at T.C.U. during his freshman year when he called persistently for books on the alcohol problem. Returning from Valparaiso, he was very active in the study group in his college, both as an undergraduate and while taking a course in law. As president of the state IPA, he visited many colleges and became noted as a speaker. He continued his service after college and gave several years in the campaigns to obtain local option and other advances in legislation. His youthful ability quickly gained public attention. He was so devoted that he over-taxed his strength, lost his health, and literally gave his life for the Cause. The Librarian at T.C.U. who had seen his devotion as a freshman then raised a fund to provide the college with a collection of up-to-date books marked, "The Wade Memorial Library".

CHAPTER V

CENTERING ON ACTION IN 1914-1918

THE THINKING AND ACTIVITIES of the Association as an American college movement, keenly conscious of the rising swell of public opinion toward removing the whole "Saloon System", may be seen in the report of the General Secretary to the National Convention at Topeka, Kansas, December 29, 1914. This was the outstanding public event in the IPA to that date.

The report specified 256 colleges and university branches, 230 of them very active, with 6,500 local members, and affirmed that "it has left its influences on nearly half of the colleges in the United States" at a period when enrollment in colleges was a small fraction of what it has been since World War II.

> These active leagues included state universities and independent church related, and small colleges. Among the large schools were Cornell, Harvard, Brown, Dartmouth, Leland, Stanford, University of Minnesota, California, Wisconsin, Iowa, Missouri, Nebraska, Ohio State, Kentucky, Georgia, Tennessee, Florida, and Washington. It was the most extensive and active intercollegiate organization of a civic character at that period in the United States.
>
> The influence of the movement in these educational institutions reached far beyond its membership. The speakers procured each year, the courses of lectures, the series of oratorical contests, the debates, discussions, open meetings, the courses of instruction initiated, often at the request of students, the activity of students in no-license and local option campaigns, the new books introduced into libraries, the educational program, and most of all, the personal work among students and the talks in conferences and chapels by the travelling secretaries sent out by the National Association, often twice a year, had been continuous through three college generations of students.

In those years the IPA was a movement of civic character that emphasized the moral responsibilities of educated men in public affairs. It sought to turn the attention of students toward leadership and service in the great problems of their own generation—to the liquor problem, as the one they surely would have to face in their day of public activity.

It educated, it appealed to the conscience, to the duty of personal service in reform. It furnished a definite field in which to apply the ideals developed in college.

Quoting again from the report: "It belongs to this student generation; it must do its work. . . . It may not be needed as a college institution ten years from now. It will not be so needed, if it does what it should now."

Citizenship Clinics

Many student leagues gained first-hand experience and greatly aided the cause in anti-saloon and no-license campaigns as poll workers, petition canvassers, speakers, and surveyors of social and political disorders connected with saloons in their towns. They prepared data for publication, and used their influence against drinking after the ball games and at banquets. The number of groups doing such work increased 30% that year.

The particular value of these activities was the experience gained with reality during the four years he was occupied with textbooks. The campaign was a citizenship clinic that trained him to be practical in after-college politics. For example, in 1913 and 1914:

The Augustana College league, Rock Island, Illinois, carried on for two years an investigation of the social conditions and political affiliations of the saloons in Rock Island and published the findings for a local option campaign.

A Harvard group had ten men in a Cambridge no-license fight in 1914.

The University of Minnesota league studied local conditions and methods of educational propaganda.

California waged a three-year campaign against drinking on the campus and did away with the "beer-busts".

The Women's League at California organized its members to bring the "California dry" issue to the women's clubs of their home communities.

Ohio State started a movement in a Columbus suburb that carried the town "dry".

Wisconsin students took part in a big saloon fight in Madison.

DePauw students kept Greencastle "dry" at one election.

At Monmouth, Illinois, eight young men aided a successful anti-saloon campaign.

Asbury College, Kentucky, sent fifty students to Frankfort to support a bill in the legislature.

Berea, Kentucky, had six men at work in nearby towns.

St. Paul College of Law aided a suburb "to go dry".

Findlay, Ohio, had twenty in a local option fight.

Oregon Agricultural circulated a voters' pledge in town and college.

Willamette, Oregon, had a part in banishing saloons from Salem, the capital city.

Gettysburg, Pennsylvania, had six in a county campaign for several weeks.

Bridgewater, Virginia, sent teams of speakers and workers into fourteen towns.

Idealism in Action

The vigor of spiritual dedication, sometimes a sacrificial devotion to the cause that had marked the first decade from 1900 among college groups, spread widely and became directly related to state and national drives toward removal of the liquor traffic then going on.

A Southern California group of forty, in 1914, led by Earl H. Haydock, University of Southern California, gave a summer and fall to the election of Charles H. Randall to Congress.

> Every morning they would assemble at a designated center, hold an informal conference, study, classify and compare the experiences and difficulties of the preceding day. After prayer they would go in a body to a suburban town, or a section of Los Angeles to carry on their canvass. They would knock at every door and ask the voters to support the proposed state constitutional amendment to make California "dry" and vote for Randall . . . . They interviewed 27,000 voters, enrolling 20,000 of them.

Randall was elected and was active for years in Washington.

In the very active years after "Valparaiso", the officers of the Association planned three large conventions, beginning with Topeka, as "West", the so-called "Prohibition Capital of the Nation", to be followed in two years by one in Lexington, Kentucky, as South, and two years later, at Cornell University, Ithica, New York, as East.

Rapid growth occurred after 1910; the number of college leagues and their activity in study and in field work practically doubled in two years. A national convention of church young people flung out a slogan, "A saloon-less nation by 1920". The IPA was not then ready to take that stand; its leaders were divided. The attitude of most of them, and of the members in the college leagues, while continuing local field service in many activities against the saloon, was that it would be wiser to concentrate longer on basic education. That slogan seemed to be super-idealistic.

Then, in November, 1913, there was held in Columbus, Ohio, a great national convention. It brought together the leaders of all the temperance and anti-alcohol organizations of America to formulate a program of united action. Sponsored chiefly by the Anti-Saloon League, the attendance was five thousand, and people came from every state in the Union. After four days of stirring public speaking, while committees debated all day until midnight, the Resolutions Committee, J. Frank Hanley, ex-governor of Indiana, chairman, presented a statement which was enthusiastically accepted by the convention:

> We therefore declare for the national annihilation, by amendment to the Federal Constitution, which shall forever inhibit throughout the territory of the United States, the manufacture, sale, importation, exportation and transportation of intoxicating liquors to be used as a beverage.

The Topeka National Convention

Early in 1914, the IPA began to organize the previously planned student convention for December of that year. It was called, as a representative college convention, to express the position of the Association in the growing public situation. The Valparaiso convention in 1910 had expressed the enthusiasm of the successful pioneer years; "Topeka" expressed the more realistic, yet highly enthusiastic attitude that had come out of successful experience and a larger vision of the future. It scored as high-point in the idealistic-emotionalism of the early years of the Association. It played up discussion, a relatively new convention technique, as well as inspirational information brought by great speakers.

The Topeka convention opened, December 29, 1914, with the two-year National Oratorical Contest. Seven interstate sections competed for national honors. Earl H. Haydock, University of Southern California, won first, and Henry C. Jacobs, Hope College, Michigan, second.

Three Kansas Governors gave addresses of welcome—George H. Hodges, retiring, Arthur Capper, incoming, and John P. St. John, former governor and "The Father of Prohibition in Kansas".

An outstanding address, "The College Student in Civic Affairs", was given by Dr. Charles M. Sheldon, author of *In His Steps,* a noted book of the century relating the personal leadership of a sacrificial minister who had devoted himself to seeking change of social conditions in the slums of a great city. The book sold extremely well.

President Colvin brought to the four hundred or more students attending from California to New Hampshire an address on "The Challenge of Today". Elmer L. Williams, called "the Fighting Parson of Chicago", who had been a member of our first student group at Gettysburg College, gave a first-hand story of his fight with vicious politics in that city. Harry G. McCain, university secretary, spoke on "The Challenge to Business and Social Welfare". Harley H. Gill, ex-traveling secretary, brought "The Challenge of the Student to This Generation", and Daniel A. Poling, vice-president, gave an outstanding address—"The Challenge of Patriotism". A letter of greeting from William J. Bryan, United States Secretary of State, was read by Elon G. Borton, secretary of the Association.

There was only one lecture from the background of scientific understanding, "Alcohol and the Physician of Today", by David Paulson, M.D., of the Hinsdale Sanatarium, Illinois. "The Women of Today" was the message brought by Mrs. Frances E. Beauchamp, a national W.C.T.U. leader from Kentucky. P. A. Baker, General Superintendent of the Anti-Saloon League of America, centered attention on "The Present National Situation" in which the trend toward Federal action had come to dominate public attention. Virgil G. Hinshaw, who had become Chairman of the Prohibition Party, gave a parallel address from the viewpoint of the party.

The following resolution expressed the spirit of the convention:

> In the future, as in the past, the greatest need will be for trained leaders. In every community, among all professions, in private as well as public life, there will be urgent need of men and women who can mould public sentiment and deepen conviction, clarify the social consciousness and vivify the public conscience.

First Ohio Campaign

In 1915 at least 650 Ohio students, 50 of them co-eds, took part in the state campaign of that year to enlarge the vote for state constitutional prohibition. Teams of two, three, or four each were formed and sent out by state or county management to hold meetings on the streets, in public halls, churches, and schoolhouses. They furnished singers, bands, and quartets for rallies; used stereopticons and posters; canvassed voters and helped them to the polls on voting day; and, in general, added the enthusiasm that stirred easy-going citizens to action.

Groups from 16 colleges reported the following data: Number of students and teachers in field work without payment for service, 650; speakers supplied for 243 meetings; singers for 172; teams of two to four each for speaking, 35; for music, 39; student speakers, 175; singers, 189; women singers, 52; students doing personal calling, or clerical work, 255; at the polls on voting days, 128. The average number per college participating was 33. These statistics are understated, rather than overstated, as several groups failed to report.

The 16 active colleges were: Adelbert, Ashland, Baldwin-Wallace, Defiance, Denison, Heidelberg, Hiram, Lane Theological, Miami, Mount Union, Oberlin, Ohio State, Ohio Northern, Ohio Wesleyan, Otterbein, and Wooster. Mt. Union had the largest number from one college, over 100; a professor was chairman of the Alliance "Ohio Dry" committee; 50 were at the polls on election day; 82 canvassed voters; two teams worked in the saloon district; speakers were supplied for 60 meetings and singers for 50.

At Western Reserve in the heart of Cleveland, 25 men were at the polls on election day; 14 canvassed voters and gave other personal aid.

Ohio State furnished 15 volunteer speakers for 17 meetings in Columbus and towns near the Capital.

Oberlin made a record with 61 volunteers, three teams and individual workers; a professor coached the men; three quartets were active; nine students were speakers, 42 canvassed voters, worked at the polls, or organized meetings.

Wooster offered two teams, who were out nearly every night for three weeks. Their program was reported to be the most effective of the campaign in Wayne County. Most of the time was given to three districts that previously had been "wet". They voted "dry". Street meetings brought out the voters in small communities, the students did the rest. There were 25 such meetings held by 15 men and 8 women, singers and speakers, 10 were at the polls on election day. A total of 30 shared in the program. A popular professor was coach.

A similar program at Ashland College was carried out by four teams, 18 men and 16 women, in street meetings from automobiles, led by a young professor. At Otterbein 20 students took part in 14 meetings; several times as many volunteered as could be accepted. Heidelberg supplied speakers for 7 meetings; music for 10, 2 quartets, 8 in personal work, and instructed voters, both in the college and outside, how to cast ballots.

At Defiance young women led off; 35 students provided music for meetings; 50 shared in the campaign, a professor was coach.

Baldwin-Wallace, with many students from German Polish families, gave pronounced support to the campaign. Their students were among the most active in the state; they provided four teams, 20 men speaking, and 28 calling on voters. Every student with a vote was reported to have voted "dry".

Twenty-six at Ohio Wesleyan furnished campaign singing, 10 did speaking, 12 personal calling, for a total of 48. Singers were supplied for a "County Dry Flying Squadron". There were so many experienced speakers in this community that student participation was limited to supplying music. Miami had six vote promoters in personal work with a faculty member as coach. Twenty-eight at Lane Theological Seminary plunged into the conflict in the "wettest" city of the state, Cincinnati, at the polls as deputy sheriffs. Speakers were supplied for 44 meetings.

At Hiram, a very small town away from saloon influence, 21 students participated, supplying speakers and music for 15 meetings in an automobile parade through the county. Denison equipped 20 meetings with speakers and singers.

Thus, 650 students of the state had a personal part, meeting people pro and con and sharing in democratic action at the base. Sometimes they cut social affairs, slighted athletic training and doubtless missed classes. By "this laboratory method" they experienced practical politics at the point where the public expresses itself. But more, they had a part as citizens in helping to determine a controversial issue, whatever the vote might show in majorities or minorities.

The Final Michigan-dry Campaign

In the summer and autumn of 1916, 600 students and faculty members participated in the state-wide campaign that resulted, in November, in a vote that adopted a prohibition amendment to the constitution of Michigan. In the previous spring a field secretary, Harry G. McCain, made a tour of the colleges, following sixteen years of annual visits by traveling secretaries of the Association. His purpose was to initiate a program similar to the one instituted in Ohio the previous year. The manager of the United Michigan Campaign, Grant M. Hudson, gave hearty cooperation and appointed Maxwell Hall of the IPA, student manager. Max began in the summer and continued through November when Michigan "went dry" by a majority of 70,000 votes.

Carefully compiled reports indicated that 524 students and 44 faculty members, 13 universities, colleges, and professional schools had shared in the campaign; about 32 per cent of these students were women. Nearly 100 more volunteered than could be used.

Thirteen colleges supplied volunteers; Adrian, Albion, Alma, Central State Normal, Ferris Institute, Hillsdale, Hope, Kalamazoo, University of Michigan, Michigan Agricultural, Michigan State Normal, Olivet, and Western State Normal.

They held 115 meetings; furnished music for 106, teams—22, quartets—27, speakers and musicians together totaled 318. The volunteers included 202 men and 69 women. Others did clerical work at headquarters, canvassed voters, watched at the polls for illegal votes, brought voters to the polls and supplied enthusiasm for parades and public demonstrations; a total of 44 faculty members and 524 students.

A Hope college reporter wrote: "The men's glee club at Hope accompanied a pageant to the five largest centers in the county drawing tremendous crowds. In Grand Haven, 1,500 attended; the crowd was so large that the floor gave way, but with no unfortunate consequences. Every school house in the county was visited."

A college band and 190 Albion students gave enthusiasm to a dry parade in Hillsdale; 300 from Ferris helped swell a parade in Big Rapids. Polls in several Michigan colleges showed that student opinion in favor of state prohibition was "overwhelming". Straw votes at the University at Ann Arbor, Hope College, Kalamazoo, and Ferris resulted in 3737 for the dry amendment to 589 against it. Hillsdale, Hope, Michigan State Normal, and Olivet reported that every voter in college voted dry; Adrian, all but one; Michigan Agricultural, 90% were for the amendment. At Adrian, the Dean of Women enlisted girls for clerical work at the headquarters. The Alma League took charge of sending out sample ballots. A Central State team held meetings throughout the rural districts—everywhere these programs were a delight to the communities. Ferris furnished 88 workers, 8 of them faculty members, 5 speaking teams, 5 quartets. From Hope 75 volunteers visited 115 school houses.

At Kalamazoo 87 assisted in canvassing unknown registrations, distributing literature, driving autos, and furnishing speakers and musicians.

Getting the students to vote by mail was the effective work at the University of Michigan. Over 120 were lined up for various kinds of work, and a training class was conducted for speakers. More could have been furnished had they been needed.

The State Normal College at Ypsilanti contributed 33 workers, 8 were members of the faculty. In addition to three speaking teams and three quartets, Olivet furnished an orchestra.

Faculty and students worked hand in hand at Western Normal School, Kalamazoo. The student body was canvassed to find eligible voters; faculty members used their cars to carry voters to the polls and others helped in clerical and personnel work. A typical celebration at Ypsilanti was staged:

> On Wednesday night after the victory was assured, 300 students got one of the big water wagons of the city and put on a "regular" dry celebration. We stopped at every saloon in town. One saloonkeeper showed fight. Another came out and told us with all sincerity, and, I believe, honesty, that he voted dry. He had a son and a brother who had begun to go down through the influence of his business.

Maxwell Hall, a secretary from the Intercollegiate Association, visited the colleges constantly, organizing and securing the co-operation of faculties and outlining programs. High testimony to the character of the work done by the college people came from Grant M. Hudson, Superintendent of the Michigan Dry Campaign Committee, who reported:

> Mr. Hall rendered most valuable service indeed, and the entire campaign conducted by your Association throughout our institutions has been of the very strongest character. We shall expect not only immediate results, but in the years to come shall look for leaders from these institutions, in various fields of life endeavor.

"Lexington, 1916"

An all-time "high" in the experience of the Intercollegiate Association in the immediate pre-prohibition period was our National Convention at Lexington, Kentucky, December 28-31, 1916. Student delegates from 25 states and 128 colleges—650 of them—from Dartmouth and Harvard to Southern California and Willamette, Oregon—expressed both the enthusiasm of the general movement in 1915-16 and the activities of the organized groups in the local colleges. A special train from Minnesota picked up delegates enroute through Chicago and Indiana.

There were two great underlying trends in the situation of those years—the steady advance of the anti-liquor movement toward national action, as shown by the rapid gains being made in local and state "dry" territory, and the election and re-election of men to Congress on national prohibition issues. Also, after 1916, there was an increasing fear that the United States might be drawn into the war in Europe.

Continuing the spirit of the Topeka Convention two years earlier, the theme of "Lexington" was "Answering the Challenge of the National Movement". A Kentucky orator, Col. George Bain, in his flowing Southern style, greeted the delegates saying:

> The South is going dry. You from the North came down and lifted the yoke of slavery off us; now if you don't be careful we will return the compliment by going up and lifting the yoke of drink off you.

After the first session with the Mayor of Lexington, Major Rogers, Col. Bain and William Jennings Bryan as the speakers, the convention gave attention each morning to sectional conferences, led by IPA secretaries on the program of the Association. "Study of the Problem", by D. Leigh Colvin, president; "The Oratorical Contests", Samuel W. Grathwell; "The Deputation Activities", Mark R. Shaw; "Publicity", John L. Warner; "Alcohol and Athletes", L. S. Reiman, top athlete at the University of Michigan; "Activities in the Large Universities", George Stewart, Yale; "College Women and Their Work", Mamie White (Mrs. D. Leigh) Colvin; "Students in State Campaigns", Maxwell Hall; "State Officers", Elon G. Borton; and "Relation of the Association to Other Organizations", Harry S. Warner.

Other outstanding addresses were by Presidents E. E. Sparks of Penn State and W. A. Ganfield of Centre, Kentucky; Charles Stelzle, expert in Labor Relations; Dr. Winfield Scott Hall, Northwestern University, physiologist, and Dr. Daniel A. Poling, Vice-President of the IPA.

The Second "Drive" in Ohio

Soon after the enthusiasm of the great Lexington Convention, and the launching of a greater program, the interest of all students as well as the public was absorbed by World War I, which had been going on in Europe for two years. The threat to the United States from German submarines became intolerable; the danger to shipping was critical. In April, 1917, the United States declared war on the Central Powers in support of France and Great Britain. Most of our field secretaries and officers were called into military service. But the coming of war only added new reason and deeper concern about the role of the liquor traffic, and the use of intoxicants by the public and in military camps. Heavier and heavier restrictions were laid on the sale of alcoholic beverages, and were followed by various forms of prohibition, including a movement to conserve food material "to win the war".

Parallel with this situation in 1917, and in continuation of long standing plans—but with a new and burning motive added—all anti-drink organizations, most churches, many newspapers and civic groups of Ohio united to press again for constitutional prohibition, a long-time struggle in the Buckeye state.

Seeking a part in "making America strong at home", while members of their own college classes were already in training camps, more than a thousand students in the autumn of 1917 took personal part in the state-wide campaign that resulted, on November 6th, in the reduction of the previous "wet" majority of 555,000 to 11,137—a decisive advance for the "dry". Two years later, state prohibition was adopted by a heavy majority.

Organization of this second, 1917, campaign of Ohio students to aid a state-wide drive for state prohibition began in April at the annual state convention of the Intercollegiate Association, at Ohio Wesleyan University, Delaware, Ohio. It took place just a few days after the United States ventured into the First World War. An enthusiastic attendance debated for three days about what students could, and should, do to give maximum service to both causes. After discussion, including many a hot debate led by a few on pacifism, a strong practical program was adopted to unite on the "wet-dry" campaign by forming thirty teams from thirty colleges by students not qualified for military service. Many state IPA officers were on the job all summer. National officers also helped. W. Willard Hall of the University of Michigan, who had much previous experience, was appointed Student Director by Superintendent James A. White of the united citizen forces who aided financially. Many students who had enrolled in the spring had been called to the army by September; however, there were more than could be used to take their places.

Reports at the end of the campaign in November showed that 960 students had taken part in field and headquarters activities, organizing public meetings and taking polls. Several colleges known to be active did not report. The estimate of 1,000 participants is a conservative one.

More student work was done in the large cities in this campaign than two years earlier, followed by changes from "wet" to "dry" when the votes were counted. "Vote getting" had been the specific purpose at Western Reserve in Cleveland, Lane Seminary in Cincinnati, Ohio State in Columbus, Bonebrake and Central in Dayton, and Wittenberg in Springfield. Baldwin-Wallace at Berea, a suburb of Cleveland, sent teams of Slavic, German, and Polish students to interview voters of their language groups in Cleveland.

At Ohio University, Athens, 20 students gave service on election day—50 in all were in the campaign. A young woman, as chairman, kept the headquarters at Athens filled with college girls. Thus, a total of 1,500 hours of political activities were given by the students of Ohio University.

War-Time Activities

Then the war put an end to all field activities of the Association. The younger secretaries—Borton, Schultz, and others—entered the Army; Schmidt became an Army YMCA secretary, Colvin a chaplain, and we who were older or ineligible shared in related war-time fields of service. The Chicago office was left in charge of a young woman secretary, and Phillips and I entered the Committee on War Temperance Activities, an agency that represented most of the temperance organizations in civilian and church war service.

The United Committee was set up in New York under the realistic vision and lead of Dr. Daniel A. Poling who had been conferring with governmental, welfare, and religious leaders in Great Britain on how to strengthen the morale of the men in the Allied Armies in France. This committee helped particularly in the American Army camps during and following the end of hostilities. Harley H. Gill, former Vice-President of the Association, was called to be Executive Secretary. Later he went overseas for two years of strenuous speaking and counseling in the camps. Another man took his place as executive; then he also went as speaker and I became the executive in New York during the period that the Army men were waiting impatiently for transportation home. The speakers the committee sent gave reports about the coming of prohibition, with factual information, to counteract a great wave of untruthful propaganda that "the wets" were trying to "put across" to restless men after the armistice.

Recalling his experiences of those strenuous days, Dr. Gill, years later, reported that many anti-prohibition propagandists speaking among the army camps had been saying, "While you boys were away fighting for freedom, a bunch of radicals put this prohibition business over on you."

Under Dr. Poling's and my own leadership, additional speakers went to France to tell the real story. "Our troops, waiting for return transportation, were an unhappy and critical lot of men, ready for almost any kind of unfavorable propaganda." Continued Mr. Gill, "I spoke night after night to hundreds of men, finding very respectful audiences, first in hotels in Paris, then in St. Nazaire, and Brest, where Navy men were coming and going and where troops from the occupation area were waiting for transportation to take them home."

CHAPTER VI

THE ORATORICAL CONTESTS OF TWENTY-SIX YEARS

THE PUBLIC SPEAKING CONTESTS of the Association were the most popular educational project for more than a quarter of a century. Organized in 1887, "by representatives from forty-four institutions of learning", the oratorical contests were usually held at Prohibition Party conventions until 1899. That year, the IPA had an independent student convention at Lake Forest College, Illinois, at the national level; D. Leigh Colvin of Ohio Wesleyan University represented Ohio. Colvin was elected President of the Association and Mattie Guild, Wheaton College, Illinois, became Secretary. That autumn they began looking for a man to become field secretary and enlarge the Association. That is where I came into the picture in 1900. Following my first organizing tour of three and a half months among central-western colleges, a large national oratorical contest was held in Chicago in June. Twelve state winners participated. From that date, the contests of the Association continued and grew for twenty-five years, until they became one of the largest public speaking series in America, at a time when public speaking and debating contests were particularly popular in intercollegiate competition. There were four levels on which to achieve honors; local, state, interstate, and national.

These IPA contests were the source of thousands of original speeches each year, written after much study and with painstaking care. For example, in the two-year period leading to the National Convention of 1914, at Topeka, Kansas, more than 1,100 speeches were written and delivered—first in the home colleges, then in fifty state contests, next in seven interstates, each including five to seven state winners, and finally in the Grand Biennial National. The average number of colleges holding locals and entering in interstates was 230 each year. Nearly 20,000 student addresses were written and delivered in these twenty-five years.

Our oratorical system grew strong without a cent of endowment or the aid of large cash awards from wealthy friends. The "regular" intercollegiate series conducted by the public speaking departments of colleges offered prizes nearly twice as large as those of the IPA and much enthusiastic publicity. It was not the prizes or the competition that made our series strong—it was the ideals in the *appeal of the subject itself for a quarter century.*

When it is noted that most of the students who entered a contest spent from two weeks to half a year reading, studying, and writing in preparation for their local, the educational value of this program will be better understood. Many times the student speakers were invited to give their speeches in home churches and community meetings of various kinds, especially those connected with the anti-alcohol movement. The state, interstate, and national honor winners frequently had opportunity to participate at conventions and in campaigns for law observance, education on the problem, and political activities. The national contests were held in connection with large national conventions in Chicago, Buffalo, Indianapolis, Columbus, Atlantic City, Minneapolis, and Des Moines.

The National Contest of 1901 at Buffalo, New York, with twelve state winners speaking, had a vast audience of perhaps 3,000, largely on account of the Pan-American World's Fair and a national conference of prohibition leaders being held in the city at that time.

Charles M. Hay, Central College, Fayette, Missouri, won the highest national honors. On returning to Central College in September, he began to organize leagues in all Missouri colleges that did not already have them, sponsored their group study program and contest and continued to lead them for five years as state president. After adding a law degree, he centered his attention on the "wet and dry" conflicts then going on. Later he gave much time to the Anti-Saloon League, was elected to the legislature and, at the time when the 18th Amendment was under discussion, was active for it as a United States Senator from Missouri.

At the National Convention of 1904 in connection with the Prohibition National Convention in Indianapolis, we took in $500.00 from ticket sales at 25 cents each. I had a suitcase at the ticket booth. The three sellers dumped the money into it, making it half full. At the hotel when the committee counted the money we found a $20 gold piece. Was it a mistake or a contribution? No one ever inquired. We decided that some wealthy person had just thrown it in as a contribution, but we never knew.

At the Minneapolis National at the University, in 1906, we had to count the complicated votes of six judges very carefully, while listening to the howling of a vast audience waiting for the decision. It took a half hour. Then President Hinshaw made the awards. After the crowd and speakers were gone, we recounted the votes and found that we had given the first place (and the gold) to the second place winner, who was by that hour taking a train to New York and Europe for the summer. To adjust the mistake we awarded two first place honors—and a "goat" to me that year.

From the top and near-top winners through the years came many of the national leaders of successive years; Hay of Missouri, Poling of Oregon, Miles of Oregon, Mamie White (Colvin) of Indiana, Lee of Oklahoma, Wideman of Florida, Ryan of Kansas, Pierce of Texas, and Grathwell of Kentucky.

Thousands of other students who participated in these contests through the years later served the anti-alcohol movement of America as educators, scientists, ministers, and in welfare, political and religious fields, as a result of the inspiration and experience gained in the oratorical contests, study classes, and field experiences made possible by the Association.

The Top Winners of Twenty-Five Years

1900—Chicago, Illinois, *Rayner W. Kelsey,* Earlham College, Richmond, Indiana. Five years in Oregon as a worker with the IPA and in the general field. While teaching at a California college, lost his job as a result of his anti-liquor activity, but immediately won a better position as Professor of History at Haverford College, Pennsylvania.

1901—Buffalo, New York, *Charles M. Hay,* Central College, Missouri, before a National Prohibition Conference and Pan-American audience of 3,000 or more. He became a state and national leader in the cause and a United States Senator.

1902—Lincoln, Nebraska, *James W. Durham,* University of Chicago, at a conference of the Intercollegiate Association won first, and Herbert A. Shattuck, Cornell University, New York, won second.

1903—Corvallis, Oregon, *Chester P. Gates,* and *Daniel A. Poling,* Dallas College, Oregon. Gates won the Western Interstate and Poling became one of the greatest public speakers and editors of the anti-alcohol movement of the century.

1904—Indianapolis, Indiana, at a National Convention of the Prohibition Party, *Walter R. Miles,* Pacific College, Oregon, first;

Mamie White, Wheaton College, Illinois, second. Miles became an outstanding psychologist as a professor at Yale University, and an international expert in research. *Mamie White* (Mrs. D. Leigh Colvin) became a life-long dedicated leader in the New York state and National Women's Christian Temperance Unions in both of which she was president. She was known particularly as a speaker and executive.

1906—Minneapolis, Minnesota, at the University of Minnesota, *Archie L. Ryan,* Baker University, Kansas, first; and *Elwood S. Minchim,* Whittier College, California, second. Ryan, a Methodist minister and administrator, spent many years in the Philippines and later in the Central West as a leader for the Cause.

1908—Columbus, Ohio, at a National Convention, *Charles S. Pierce,* Howard Payne College, Texas, first; *Levi T. Pennington,* Earlham College, Indiana, second. Pierce became a leader in state-wide activities. Pennington became a college president and a devoted leader for the cause in Oregon.

1910—Valparaiso, Indiana, at the National Convention of the IPA. First, *Laurel E. Elam,* Greenville College, Illinois, who became a prohibition supporter and lawyer in Idaho, and second was *Lewis M. Simes,* Southwestern College, Kansas, who was active in his state.

1912—Atlantic City, New Jersey, at a National Convention of the Anti-Saloon League. First, *Frank Wideman,* Stetson University, Florida, later an orator and political leader for state prohibition. Second, *Harry G. McCain,* Willamette University, Oregon, Vice-President of the IPA and, later, a political leader in Alaska.

1914—Topeka, Kansas, at the National Convention of the Intercollegiate Association. First honors went to *Earl H. Haydock,* University of Southern California, who is dedicated to the cause and is still working at it. Second was *Henry C. Jacobs,* Hope College, Michigan. He was active in the following years and served with the IPA to 1964.

1916—Lexington, Kentucky, at the National Student Convention of the Association. First honors, *Joshua B. Lee,* University of Oklahoma. He became a United States Senator in the testing years, "the twenties". Also *Bernard C. Clausen,* Colgate University, New York, one of the outstanding Baptist ministers of the country.

1919—Des Moines, Iowa, January 5, 1920, at a National Convention of the IPA. First, *Margaret Garrison,* Willamette University, Oregon, the first woman to win the highest honors in the contests of the Association. Second, *Henry K. Cassidy,* Ottawa University, Kansas, who won his entry previous to World War I. He became a Captain in the U.S. Army and gained oratorical honors in this final National of the IPA series of oratorical contests.

This National Contest at Des Moines, held just as constitutional prohibition was coming into effect, included three speakers who had won their local, state, and interstate honors before entering the Army, the others won during the war.

The oration of Miss Margaret Garrison, class of 1920, "A New Reconstruction", was both a paean of victory expressing the majority sentiment of the students of that year and an understanding of the serious responsibility that would have to be faced in the very near future as she said:

> Half a century ago America faced one of the greatest crises of its history. It was to determine not whether the nation could exist "half slave and half free", but whether it could exist at all. Then came the memorable day at Appomattox, with the high assurance to a people unified and purified by infinite sacrifice, that they should not perish from the earth. The cancerous growth of slavery was removed, but the weakened, bleeding, impoverished nation did not soon recover. There followed the fever and delirium of the reconstruction period; the awful tragedy in Ford's Theatre, the shameful spoilation of the Carpetbagger, the terror of the Ku Klux Klan. Can we ever forget it? Can we ever cease to wonder that we did survive? In the bitterness of mistake and sorrow, America was taught that every revolution must be followed by a period of reconstruction.
>
> Now we are on the threshold of a similar crisis. The echoes of Armageddon are dying away. The threatening thrones of autocracy are falling to destruction, and we are entering into a new sense of security in our democracy. Like unto our success abroad, and associated with it, has been the victory at home over the formidable foe—Alcohol. Like the last of the Caesars, like slavery, "King Alcohol" has been defeated and dethroned in the seven-fold fires of a mighty revolution. But in our exultation over victory, we should not be unmindful of the lessons of other days. We

should remember that the destruction of any institution requires a corresponding readjustment. As "King Alcohol" retreats there is need for a realignment of certain factors in the economic and social interests of men. Unless wise foresight be exercised, unless a sane reconstruction be affected, there will be loss, turmoil and antagonism.

There are always two forces contending in nature; one organizing, the other disorganizing. Vital energies seeking to build up are forever opposed by forces which would tear down. The liquor interests do not calmly accept their defeat and it is not natural that they should. Have not these men invested their means and very lives in a business which has utterly been destroyed? Have not many believed the liquor industry legitimate, and others contended that they have a right to direct their personal habits? It does not obviate the results of their belief to say that they were in error. The serious fact that they so believe is there—a stinging source of bitterness and opposition. How shall their problem with its human resistance be treated?

We stand for prohibtion with all that its name implies. But law is not dynamic; no law will enforce itself.

Thus, Margaret Garrison, student speaker of 1918, gave to the convention her prophecy of the future.

Chapter VII

CONSTRUCTIVE SERVICE IN "THE TWENTIES"

IT WAS A DECIDEDLY NEW and unknown future that confronted the Intercollegiate Association, January 5, 1920, as it met in convention in Des Moines, Iowa, just eleven days before *National Prohibition* came into effect as the Constitutional method of dealing with the problem of Alcohol in the future.

A spirit of victory and adventure prevailed. A great social welfare movement had taken a long step forward. The reduction of drunkenness and the beginnings of alcoholism could now be undertaken with confidence. Indeed, surveys and tests, compiled three to five years later, show these desirable results actually followed to a much greater extent than the public knew. Yet, underneath the dominate sense of optimism and confidence at the time, there was a feeling of concern that the task, well begun, was far from finished. Our more idealistic idealists, who believed that the government could do everything, had been a bit too idealistic.

The Association had now completed nineteen and one-half years of organized activity. Just before America entered World War I, the IPA was the largest student movement of a civic character in the country. During the war, the attention of the generation in college and of recent graduates was absorbed in that deadly conflict. Immediately after it ended, we all faced a decidedly new outlook and a new question. What influence would these two major world events, the 18th Amendment and the World War, have on the struggle of a century to reduce drunkenness? What influence would the strength of the alcohol industry and the social drinking culture have on this struggle?

> The National Conference at Des Moines was called "to discuss, first the helping to make the new law and policy a fact in the social and economic life of the people, and then, to consider the possibilities of friendly cooperation with students in other lands in the growing fight against alcohol the world around."

The Convention faced frankly the fact that the anti-alcohol movement in the United States was far from complete, that ". . . large elements of the people must yet be brought into sympathetic support." Nor did it fail to recognize that within the next few years they, themselves, would have the opportunity—and the serious responsibility—of helping to make the new solution a reality in the life of the nation. "Des Moines" did not overlook, although perhaps it could not appreciate it, the long-time education that would be necessary to change the attitudes and customs of "those who were not convinced" sufficiently to make this new approach a solution even to the legal, much less the social aspects of the problem. In this it only shared with many others who expected law to do more than law could do.

At the same time, it did see with collegiate idealism an outlook for cooperation with non-drinking movements in the universities and colleges of other countries and a forecast of the position that the United States would occupy in world affairs as a result of having made this country a huge laboratory for testing one of the greatest social welfare experiments in the history of nations—the attempt to banish intoxicating drink by legal democratic action.

To this convention of representative students in 1920, and to many thoughtful people in other countries, America's adoption of prohibition and the heavy restrictions laid on the sale of liquor by Great Britain, Canada, Germany, and France as war time measures, had made the problem of alcohol and alcoholism one on which youth and students could work together in many countries to advance friendship between nations as a "moral equivalent for war".

College Visitation Continued

The personal contact of the secretaries of the Association with colleges had been the most direct and effective form of activity through the previous twenty years of this project. It was continued as fundamental to the future. The secretaries were recent students, a year or two or three out of college. They shared the attitudes, sympathies, and prejudices of their period. They understood the changes in student psychology that occur from one college generation to another. They spent from two to three days at a college conferring with group leaders, studying campus problems, sharing discussions, speaking in chapels, and organizing programs. They carried the story of what was being said and done from one college to another and from state to state.

This service was continued through the thirteen years of the national experiment. The number of IPA secretaries employed varied from two to seven per year. In 1923, they visited 200 colleges; in 1924, 174 in 16 states; in 1925, 231; and in 1926, 164 colleges in 17 states. In the year ending in June, 1928, 412 different colleges received a total of 507 visits in this direct and personal way. Because of their persistent efforts to approach the problem of law observance, very acute at that time, they were received heartily by presidents, deans, and student organizations.

Literature of the Period

During 1923 and after, the Association published reports of changing attitudes among colleges and such pamphlets as: "What University Athletes Say" by L. C. Reiman, University of Michigan, athlete, five printings; "Has Prohibition Improved Conditions as to Drink Among College Students?", a survey; "College Student Editors on College Student Drinking"; "Student Opinion Expressing Itself on Law Observance, Prohibition and Ideals Back of Prohibition"; "Have Five Years Produced Results?", opinions of presidents; "Why Prohibition?", a syllabus for discussion (pro and con) of controverted phases; "Nationalism and Alcoholism in Japan" by Joseph Tatsuro Santo; "The Threshold of a New Era" and "An Appeal to the Students of the World" by Dr. Courtney C. Weeks, London; "Changing Student Customs" and "A Constructive Equivalent For War" by Harry S. Warner. A series of twenty posters on law observance and citizenship with statements by the President of the United States, the Chief Justice of the Supreme Court, economists, sociologists, and athletes were posted on the bulletin boards of 130 colleges, weekly for four years.

Enlarging Educational Activities

Continuously through the thirteen years of the prohibition experiment, the Association promoted study of the progress—and lack of progress—being made from year to year in public opinion and social customs relating to the alcohol problem. It soon became evident that much change in the deeper strata of public opinion would have to accompany effective support of the ideals implied in legal banishment.

As a first step in this direction, the IPA organized tours for speakers to clarify and emphasize the philosophy of and respect for the law, and of all law as such. Dr. Elwood Perisho, President of State College, South Dakota; Dr. Ira Landreth, President of the IPA; Rev. Elmer L. Williams, "Fighting Parson", from the downtown precincts of Chicago where the violation of any law became a form of racketeering, were engaged as speakers to visit college campuses, with sessions of one to several days each.

Writing and research contests were promoted at national and foreign student levels. In 1922, students of 19 nationalities in 130 North American colleges participated, the theme being "The World Movement Against Alcoholism". Four cash prizes totaling $1,000 were awarded by the World League Against Alcoholism at the Toronto Convention of 1942 to Frank H. Nelson, University of Chicago, first; J. N. Sahni of India, attending the University of Michigan, second; and Hannah Jane Starr, Queen's University, Kingston, Ontario, Canada, third. A National Award a year later brought papers from sixty-eight colleges in 26 states, prizes $1,050; John Clark, Lenox College, Iowa, won first honors.

Introducing Forum Discussion

The Forum Discussion Method to encourage free expression of conflicting views on public questions was popular at this time. Our secretaries began to emphasize this procedure as an educational technique in dealing with enforcement. From the beginning of the prohibition period, the IPA placed emphasis on the free discussion of all opinions, reports of success and failure, and the principles of the anti-alcohol movement. Within two years, 200 colleges and universities had such discussions, led by well-balanced speakers. In 1926, one leader visited 28 universities and colleges in seven weeks, led 55 forums, and addressed 5,450 students. After one visit, he reported that:

> . . . at one of the wettest fraternities, we sat down and talked the matter over for two hours—twenty-six students and myself. They were very cordial, but not friendly to prohibition. They criticized freely; they told of bootleggers that come to student houses; of where the fellows get it; boasted how they did it. They believed conditions to be worse than they used to be. But after talking it over frankly, after they had a chance to see what "the old days" (five years before) were like, one fellow said, "How old were we when Prohibition was adopted?" In that talk, they thought the question through for themselves and convinced themselves.

Foreign Students in American Colleges

Much attention was given after 1918 to the students from foreign lands who were attending colleges and universities in the United States. They numbered around 10,000, from 60 or more different countries, and represented 95 nationalities. Of these, there were 25 from Australia; 21 from Austria; 28 from Belgium; 23 from Bulgaria; 37 from Denmark;

170 from England; 38 from Scotland; 97 from South Africa; 101 from Armenia; 708 from Japan; 231 from India; 58 from Norway; 18 from New Zealand; 391 from Russia; 36 from Switzerland; 58 from Sweden; 36 from Turkey; and with every country in South America included, as well as Central Asia, Africa, and the islands of the seas.

This number was very small compared with those in the following years, but it was very significant that they could see for themselves for three to five years the operations of the new American experiment during its first few years.

Chinese students in American colleges, as early as 1920, organized on their own initiative to create public opinion in America to help China head off the brewers who were sending capital and machinery to open up a market for beer in China to replace the one lost at home. They held protest conferences, issued a public statement and worked with influential people at home as well as in the United States to support their protest.

That same year, Latin American students in New York formed a group for study and discussion of liquor banishment as related to the future of their home lands.

Research and writing contests, open only to students from other countries attending colleges in the United States, were held in 1922, 1926, and 1927. In the first, 17 countries were represented—Australia, China, Japan, Siam, Yugoslavia, Holland, Sweden, Korea, Philippines, Romania, Egypt, Armenia, Bolivia, Brazil, India, Switzerland, and South Africa.

The winner was Oswald Goulter of Australia. On his return home, he was given many opportunities to speak. Second honors were awarded to Colbert N. Kurokawa, Japanese, who later became a YMCA secretary in Hawaii; third was Isabella Bu, India, who was interested in the movement in her country.

The contest of 1926 included students from 29 different countries, one reporting his nationality, "homeless". The contest of 1927, with writers from 32 countries, awarded the five highest of twenty prizes to J. D. H. Donnay, Belgium; Hsiao-Hung of China; Jeremiah W. Moore of British Guiana; George E. Gooderham of England; and George E. Zachariades of Greece.

These activities suggest the influence that the cooperation of the Association had with students from foreign lands in the prohibition years. While here for four years, they observed America critically; they judged the outlook at first hand; they went back, either favorable or antagonistic, to become educators, government officials, and business and public leaders in many lands around the world. They went either to help reduce alcoholism at home or to criticize this "great American experiment" as of no lasting value.

Early Opinions of College Officials

Very soon after the prohibition law went into effect, January 16, 1920, too soon to expect much change from previous attitudes, the Association sent a letter on March 3, 1922 to the presidents of the colleges of the country, seeking the reactions of these officials to the situation in college communities after the first two years.

The question was: "What do the faculty and students of your institution and your college acquaintances think of prohibition in theory and fact?" One hundred and fifty-eight answers were received: 136 favorable, 10 non-committal, 8 unfavorable, and 4 favorable to the theory but unfavorable to the enforcement laws.

While limited in number, the answers did come from every type and standard of college, independent universities and the state and church-related colleges. They came from 40 of the 48 states and represented every class of social, religious, and economic background. The replies showed care in preparation and analysis as illustrated by the following:

> An overwhelming majority approved both in theory and in operation and expressed their opinions in no uncertain language. Of the 136 endorsing, 65% stated that their students and faculties were almost unanimous for it.
>
> Almost universal was the opinion of these answering presidents that drinking in colleges was less than in pre-prohibition days, including several who were opposed to prohibition.
>
> "The whole problem of discipline has been both simplified and lessened," wrote the head of a great school of technology.
>
> "There is less drinking in this part of the country than ever before in the history of man," said a president, in a state that did not ratify the amendment.
>
> "In this city of 45,000 people, I have not seen an open saloon nor a drunken man in three years," said the president of a college in central Illinois.
>
> "The abolition of the American saloon is a great boon; the difficulties which are now surrounding administration of the law will gradually disappear," stated the president of a state university.

"Even lax enforcement of the law cannot obscure its value," voiced another.

"We had to get rid of the saloon, for it had become a plague spot."

"Not as successful as might be desired, but as successful as might be expected."

"Has performed miracles in closing saloons and reducing a habit so widely prevalent."

"Our campus considers community prohibition a failure; however, none would wish to go back to the old days."

"We recognize that society is better off without the organized liquor traffic."

"We do not yet see that there is a very great deal of difference in the actual amount of drinking done," said a president in Maine.

But, another Maine president said, "The present enforcement of the law in this state is better than it has been for many years."

One university head thought the "purpose desirable, but the amendment premature."

"Circumstances conspired to put the amendment into the Constitution from five to ten years too soon," a New York and a Tennessee president agreed.

"Several members of the faculty with whom I have talked," said a technical college man in Brooklyn, "believe with me that prohibition in theory, if light wines and beer had not been excluded, is a good thing but, in fact, there has been more drinking than before."

From the heart of New York City, a president said, "The students overwhelmingly approve it, the faculty are a little further from unanimity."

"There is no such fact . . . the laws are not enforced, most people think they cannot be enforced. Others think they may be obeyed in some remote . . . future, after education has done its work," said a Tennessee president.

"Far from being a success," said a state college president in New Mexico.

"While it is true that . . . bootlegging is done, people brew their own to some extent; it is not to be compared to the old days," said another.

"The faculty and students of Northwestern University believe that no form of crime has ever been reduced so rapidly as that of drunkenness. People still carry concealed weapons . . . steal and drink, but drinkers are being reduced in number much faster than the other classes of law breakers."

The president of a college of technology in the greatest distilling center in America said, after a faculty meeting, "Our students would be nearly unanimous in the feeling that prohibition is the right condition for this country and that there should be no disturbance over the laxity in enforcement."

"It is working well from a university view-point. . . . The whole problem of discipline has been both simplified and lessened; the morale of student bodies improved and the number of men dropped because of misconduct greatly reduced."

The answers to this questionnaire were published and distributed among the colleges of the United States and sent to educational institutions in Europe. Calls for quantities came from London and Australia. Similar inquiries among deans, students, and presidents followed in 1925 and 1926. One report was translated by a professor at the university of Leipzig for German speaking countries.

Accepted as Welfare Advance

The colleges of the United States, on the whole, accepted prohibition as a social welfare advance. There were exceptions, decided and outstanding, but they were exceptions. Secret drinking continued, then became open; there was bootlegging and rum-running by students in universities near the Canadian line; there were moonshine stills in the mountains. To purchase from illegal sellers, in time, became an adventure. Student drinking and law evasion were publicized as student carousals had been in saloon days. Yet, as in license days, drinking and law violation in colleges were much less than outside. The main body of college students accepted the purposes of the new laws, agreed that alcoholic drinks were not necessary, and that eventually the customs would be outgrown.

Majority Student Support

Evidence of this trend, in the first five to seven years, is found in many surveys and tests of opinion and practice, the most scientific, though not the earliest of which was by Professor E. Everett Cortright, New York University, in 1926. His "objective evidence", Professor Cortright believed had "more than the average amount of legitimate findings in it . . . because of the manner in which it was collected." Two questions were merged with thirty-four others of large social importance. The method was sampling by classes from one to four in each of the colleges listed. The answers were as follows:

1. Should the Eighteenth Amendment be rigidly enforced?

Mt. Holyoke College group	97% Yes
Stanford University group	94% "
University of Minnesota group	88% "
Connecticut College group	87% "

	University of Michigan group	84% "
	Washington Square, N.Y.U., group	80% "
	Smith College group	70% "
	Education, N.Y.U. group	68% "
	Amherst College group	64% "
	University of Texas group	64% "
	University of North Carolina group	72% "
	Commerce, N.Y.U. group	72% "
	Average all-college groups surveyed	77% "
2.	Should the Eighteenth Amendment be abolished?	
	University of Minnesota group	90% No
	Mt. Holyoke group	83% "
	University of Michigan group	82% "
	University of North Carolina group	81% "
	Connecticut College group	70% "
	Smith College group	70% "
	Stanford University group	69% "
	Education, N.Y.U. group	68% "
	University of Texas group	68% "
	Commerce, N.Y.U. group	56% "
	Amherst College group	50% "
	Average all-college groups surveyed	69% "

"Analysis of the vote shows two distinct things. First, the wide range of regional opinion . . . the Atlantic seaboard wet . . . great Saharas in the western part of the country." Second, the effect of sex opinion upon the decisions, for to produce the average of 77% "yes" on the first question, the men gave a 66% "yes" voted and the women an 83% "yes". On the second question, to produce the 69% "no" average, the men voted 56% and the women 72% "no". The sex balance of all students recorded is practically identical with the proportionate number of men and women students in the country.[1]

Two years earlier, in 1923 and 1924, organized college groups throughout the country had begun to give public expression to their views on the questions connected with the Eighteenth Amendment.

This action was spontaneous and widespread. It seemed to mean that the students then in college were thinking of America's experiment, to free a nation of 112,000,000 people from intoxicating drink, as *one of the big ideas of the day*—as students of today think of world peace, desegre-

1. This material was presented at a hearing before the Judiciary Committee of the United States Senate in 1927. See *The International Student,* May, 1927, for a larger report.

gation of the races, and other current issues to which youth of foresight cannot avoid giving serious attention.

A Yale meeting of 2,000, in 1923, in behalf of law observance, was sponsored by *The Yale News* with Admiral William L. Sims the speaker. The February 8, 1924, *Yale News* stating editorial policy, listed as "No. 1", "The 18th Amendment should be strictly enforced throughout the university."

At Illinois College, the student body put the college on record as opposed to the current jokes on drinking in the movies, on the stage, and in college publications. It expressed strong support of the laws and sent the statement to President Coolidge. Three fraternities at Rutgers filed voluntary statements favoring prohibition and expressing intention to do all in their power to stop the use of liquors in their groups. Every fraternity reported regulations against drinking.

A national student conference in 1923 called on student bodies throughout the country for positive expression of opinions on the question. Approving this action, the *Brown University News,* January 22, 1924, reported "Already over 100 important educational institutions have voiced their approval of the enforcement of the 18th Amendment. Brown University should be added to this continually increasing list." *Hoya,* Georgetown University, Washington, D. C., editorially challenged collegians to set a national example, saying "The work might well begin in our schools, colleges, and universities." A Princeton student forum after a two-hour discussion voted for support, 192 to 42. The University of Pennsylvania class of 1925 voted dry festivities for Junior Week, the secretary of the class stated that this voiced ". . . not only its policy, but that of the entire student body." At the University of Michigan, a program prepared in anticipation of the Junior Prom included a conference of representative students, a mass meeting with student speakers, and the cooperation of fraternities. "The campus was so dry," said the *Michigan Daily,* "that they had to get out the lawn sprinklers." A straw vote "showed comfortable majorities against repeal, against the sale of beer and wine and in favor of strict enforcement."

By 1924, student groups in many colleges, large and small, began on their own initiative to express themselves against the spirit of evasion and violation of the state and national laws that supported the Prohibition Amendment. Action was being taken at the local and regional levels that showed positive support, but at the same time recognized the danger in the growing disregard and violation of law.

Five citizenship conferences, in 1923-24, brought the question of correct attitudes straight to the front as one that could not be taken lightly—*Washington, D. C.,* October 13-15, 1923. The student section of a National Citizenship Conference, with college, university, and preparatory students and recent alumni from forty colleges, called for action as follows:

> That all student bodies throughout the nation be urged . . . to express their positive stand on the question whether good citizenship does not require the unqualified observance of all law, in letter and spirit, as such observance relates particularly to the question of the enforcement of the Federal prohibition law.

Boston, Mass., January 19-21, 1924, a New England Conference at Phillips Brooks House, Harvard, 102 delegates from 22 institutions: Yale, Harvard, Massachusetts Tech., Boston, Dartmouth, Brown, Wesleyan, Wellesley, Simmons, Radcliff, Mount Holyoke, Hartford Theological, Connecticut, and Bates. The findings were expressed by the resolutions adopted:

> "*Whereas,* we believe that the question of student drinking is not entirely a moral issue but is essentially a *legal* one, involving as it does the observance and the enforcement of an integral part of the Constitution of the United States.
>
> *Be it resolved* that we as college men and women shall personally make evident our disapproval of student drinking in college dormitories, clubs and fraternity houses, and especially at college functions.
>
> That the various colleges be urged to take a definite stand against all drinking through their respective Christian associations, student councils, or governing bodies, and college publications.
>
> That arrangements be made with the Intercollegiate Prohibition Association whereby copies of these findings will be transmitted to the officers of the classes and other student activities, the faculties and the alumni of colleges and universities throughout the United States."
>
> —M. L. Umpleby, Wesleyan University, Chairman

Philadelphia, Pa., January 13, 1924, at the University of Pennsylvania, delegations from nineteen colleges of the state, New Jersey, and New York prepared findings that condensed read:

> . . . that each delegation to this conference constitute (a committee) on its own campus . . . for the express purpose of aiding law enforcement . . . and building up respect for and obedience to law . . . urge the faculty body responsible . . . or the student council if it has the power,

> to punish student offenders in the matter of intoxicants . . . faculty members to avoid cynical references to the Eighteenth Amendment . . . college authorities urged to hold fraternities responsible for the action of their alumni while in fraternity houses.

It was signed by the committee: Homer H. Hazel, Rutgers; Chris Hauson, Gettysburg; Donald Stevens, Yale; P. M. Malin, University of Pennsylvania; J. H. Jackson, Lafayette; and N. S. Hibshman, Penn State.

A conference in Washington, D. C., April 2-6, 1924, was attended by 155 undergraduates from 80 colleges and states from Texas and Colorado to New England. They discussed "The Situation in the College Today", "Shall the 18th Amendment be Nullified by a Law-Defying Minority?", "Shall the Law be Modified or Repealed?" and "Can a Government of Free Men Secure Obedience to Laws Legally Passed by a Majority?". These conferences on "Law Observance", formulated and gave national expression to the opinion of the average student at that time.

Continuation and transmitting committee: A Joint Transmitting Committee voted as follows:

> Representing the Continuation Committees of the above national and intercollegiate student citizenship conferences we hereby transmit to the student bodies of the United States the findings and resolutions with the urgent suggestion that definite action be taken at once in all colleges, through student governing bodies, student councils, representative organizations and student publications, toward the expression of a positive stand on the questions involved, in such ways as may be most suitable to conditions in the respective student committees throughout the country.

This was signed by the Committee: W. W. Dulles, Princeton; Patrick Murphy Malin, University of Pennsylvania; John P. Hubbard, Harvard; Elizabeth McDougall, Connecticut College; and Howard A. Kester, Lynchburg College.

The Syracuse University Council, aroused by the rum-running across the border from Canada, was more positive than the average. On January 7, 1924, it voted as follows:

> Whereas there has been a wave of lawlessness, especially in the evasion of the 18th Amendment sweeping over the country, and to a certain extent has made itself manifest in the colleges . . . be it resolved that the Senior Council of Syracuse University go on record as bitterly resenting this lack of law observance in our country . . . that the Senior Council very emphatically urges that each individual student in our University put himself on record as solidly behind the cause of law enforcement.

Two years later, 1928, James J. Britte, Chief Counsel of the Bureau of Prohibition in Washington, wrote ". . . the colleges, universities, and schools, with rare exceptions, are fully in line."

It was not until after 1928 that any marked deterioration in support of the prohibition policy was felt at the college level, as it had earlier at the general public level.

Ninety-Nine College Campus Tour

Organized as a team, three leaders of the Association in 1930-31 carried through a campus program of one to three days each in 99 colleges. The main speaker was Ben H. Spence of Toronto, Canada, journalist and life-long leader in the anti-alcohol movements of North America. With him on the team as student associates were Miss Ruth G. Lockman and John H. Shouse, the latter, a graduate that year of Berea College, Kentucky.

Mr. Spence specialized on "Canada's Liquor System". Ruth and John led a full program of discussion groups. There always stood out the burning issue of repeal or support of the way the law was operating—or failing to operate—and the principles back of the whole movement.

The team visited 99 colleges and universities the first year, from the University of Maine at Orono to Kansas State at Manhatten. Students, faculty members, and the general public were very responsive. Interest was high and each of the several days on a campus was filled with group conferences, lectures, and personal interviews.

At Ohio State University, the three IPA speakers shared in forty-seven faculty and student meetings and conferences for three days. At Yale, Mr. Spence led forums and conferences for two days; Pennsylvania State College, two days; Kansas State College, three days. Other universities in the program included Johns Hopkins, Boston University, Massachusetts Institute of Technology, Duke, Lafayette, American, DePauw, Indiana, Miami of Ohio, and the Universities of Wisconsin, Kansas, and North Carolina.

Thus, just before the final drive for repeal of the Prohibition policy, the IPA was meeting another crisis in our sphere of education, just as public opinion was seen to be heading toward repeal of the Eighteenth Amendment. In the one year, 1927-28, the Association sponsored 507 one-to-four day campus seminars and lecture programs in 165 colleges and universities in 34 states. These yielded chapel addresses attended by 60,866 people; lectures with discussion in 388 class sessions, attendance of 10,980, and 460 in forum groups, attendance 15,200; groups in fraternities, 184 meetings off-campus, attendance 17,329. All were accompanied by personal dicussions with faculty members and plans for follow-up programs.

Enlarging Campus Visitation

Seldom if ever in the college visitation program of the years since 1900 did a field secretary of the Association create more stirring interest among students in the four months he was with us than did W. A. C. Hughes, Jr., a law college graduate, in his intensive campaign among Negro colleges. In this period, Hughes led discussion groups and gave addresses in chapel in thirty-five colleges. He specialized and shared, as a faculty speaker and leader, in discussion of the problem in five ten-day conferences of pastors and church workers, reaching the coming leaders of his race throughout the South. In his up-to-date educational approach to the alcohol problem, his work was exceptional. Students liked him because he discussed freely with them and professors appreciated his abundant information and undogmatic appeal.

One of the most effective secretaries of the Association in the receding years of the Prohibition Era was Ruth G. Lockman of Winthrop College, North Carolina. She devoted four full years to group discussions and speaking in women's and in co-educational colleges. She had graduated from Winthrop just one year earlier and was an outstanding student leader. Miss Lockman had been president of the largest college YWCA in the country, 1500 members, delegate to and leader in state and national conferences, and was active among southern student groups who were seeking to overcome race prejudice. Miss Lockman visited an average of 100 colleges a year for four years in 19 states; she gave addresses in eighty chapels to 19,800 students, talks with discussion in 170 class sessions, led forums and conferences, and, in addition, included 41 similar meetings in off-campus conferences with young people. With her keen mind, vital, attractive personality, and sympathetic understanding, she successfully handled the sharp differences of conflicting personal attitudes toward drinking as she did with those on the problems of race.

Testing Knowledge and Attitudes

A new and direct plan to learn the attitudes of college students to the alcohol problems in the late "twenties" was begun in 1927, just as the criticism of the Eighteenth Amendment in colleges began to head toward repeal, as it had a year earlier in the general community. It was a knowledge—attitude—opinion questionnaire, prepared by Lofton S.

Wesley, Executive Secretary, and George A. Douglas, Field Secretary, in cooperation with professors of education and psychology in several colleges. The questionnaire was scientifically designed to bring out just what students were thinking about the problem and the degree of awareness, or lack of concern and understanding, that prevailed at that period. The plan was organized to include thousands of students in hundreds of colleges and to furnish data that would be a basis for instruction by teachers in their classes and discussion by groups and in creating programs that would realistically fit the immediate need. Unfortunately it had to be discontinued after only a few months on account of the great depression. Funds could not be found to make it nationwide on the scale on which it had been organized.

College Support Continued Longer

Notwithstanding their strong desire to uphold the reputation of their students and administrations, college presidents are scientific men who know how to sift evidence. The following, therefore, is of merit as showing the situation in many colleges in 1930, when "prohibition at its worst" was soon to be followed by repeal and new methods of handling the problem.

A questionnaire, in February, 1930, sent exclusively to presidents of state universities and the larger colleges, brought replies from 31 universities. Of these, 26 presidents stated their belief that student drinking was not general; only one said that there was more drinking at that time than before prohibition; 17 recorded themselves as against repeal; one favored repeal; 5 desired modification of the law; one was for modification after prohibition had been given a fair trial; one said that although drinking had decreased, the students of his institution drank hard liquors almost exclusively; one declined to answer. The conclusion seemed clear. In the experience of these administrators, there was decidedly much less drinking among colleges under prohibition than in earlier years.

By college generations, freshmen in 1926 to 1928, the graduates of 1930 to 1932 had been children in 1918. They had experienced little of the saloon; they knew less of the organized traffic and its encouragement of law defiance and vicious politics in the previous years of the saloons. Nor had they shared in scientific instruction on the problem during their youth in any way comparable with that which prevailed in the pre-prohibition years. But they knew the bootlegger, the rum-runner; they had seen all too often the evasion and defiance of law enforcement measures. They were a new generation facing different alcohol problems in the midst of a great experiment to reduce consumption that was far from completion.

Paul N. Guthrie, of the University of Tennessee, class of 1927, after traveling three years among the colleges as an IPA secretary, exchanging personal observations with thousands of students in the Eastern and Southern states, expressed a reasonable opinion of college student attitudes just before repeal of the Eighteenth Amendment when he said:

> During the last ten years, those opposed to the use of and traffic in alcoholic beverages have confined their attention too much to the Eighteenth Amendment and the Volstead Act. Their discussions tend to give the impression that the only thing needed to emancipate society from drink is to enforce these laws. Law seems to be a panacea for all the ills of alcoholism . . . a basic philosophy or force to be applied to a great problem.[2]

Thus, from students of that crisis period came a forecast of a new and deeper understanding that grew strong in the next fifteen years of the Intercollegiate Association history.

2. "More than Law", *The International Student,* March, 1929.

Chapter VIII

PARALLEL STUDENT IDEALS IN EUROPE

CORRESPONDING GENERALLY with the origin and growth of organized interest among American college students in the anti-alcohol movement, in 1900 and the years thereafter, had been similar student activities and clubs in some of the institutions of higher learning in various European countries.

On the Continent, there were local groups or clubs formed even earlier by students who wished to maintain for themselves and to promote "Temperance"—some in the sense of restraint or "moderation", the majority in the sense of "total abstinence". They had in common the desire to refuse to participate in the almost overwhelming pressure of the ancient drink traditions that dominated the customs in nearly all institutions of higher learning.

More widely than was known in the rapidly growing anti-alcohol movements of North America were educational organizations at the higher level that were giving particular attention to the problems of students as widely scattered as England and southeast Europe. There were student organizations in Holland, the Scandinavian countries, and central Europe as well as instruction in other countries.

Great Britain and the Scandinavian countries had educational organizations that specialized in promoting scientific study and provided specialists as lecturers. From his headquarters in London, Dr. Courtney C. Weeks, M.D., Army surgeon in the First World War, Anglican minister, and scientific writer, was giving full time as lecturer and organizer of instruction in teachers' colleges, seminaries, universities, and other schools of high standing throughout Great Britain.

Outstanding among the thinkers of Great Britain in the years just after World War I was Gilbert Murray, Oxford professor and historian, who had called the adoption of the Prohibition idea in America "The greatest social experiment of modern times". In a publication of the Encyclopedia Britannica, "These Eventful Years", he referred to it as one of the three greatest events of the generation that witnessed the

World War: (1) The advance of air transportation, (2) The creation of a League of Nations, and (3) The adoption of Prohibition by America! From the viewpoint of history, he suggested that the last was the greatest of the three.

Throughout all Europe this dramatic attempt of the United States to reduce and ultimately eliminate the evils of drunkenness by law produced strong opposition and questioning. An idealistic minority in nearly all countries approved; a heavy majority disapproved, but the vast intermediate section would not believe it could happen.

In academic fields, after the shock of amazement to the majority and the happy appreciation of the reformers at both faculty and student levels, discussion led to careful study, then to much "personal liberty" and emotional reaction. Not satisfied with the mass of both favorable and sarcastic reports that were coming across the Atlantic, various academic agencies wanted to know more of how students and their teachers in the colleges were taking it, and why?

Early in 1920, at the invitation of the British, Swedish, Swiss, and Dutch student and university non-drinking leaders, I was sent as a representative of the Intercollegiate Association on a tour among representative institutions of higher learning to explain objectively the history and motivation of the movement that had just culminated in the prohibition policy. Resigning the position of General Secretary in favor of a younger man, I was elected International Education Secretary. Mrs. Warner accompanied me; we sailed April 2nd and returned in December.

During the eight months, we attended conferences and summer schools, had personal conferences with professors, leaders of organized student activities, and teachers in universities and colleges in England, Scotland, Belgium, Holland, Denmark, France, Italy, Finland, and, particularly, in Sweden and Switzerland. We shared in conferences in a wide range of educational institutions, reporting on "the coming of prohibition in the United States", and the reforms that were expected to follow.

Reporting on "The American Experiment"

This extended tour followed a series of lectures and conferences in Belgium, England, Scotland, and France by D. Leigh Colvin, in 1919, President of the Association, while a Chaplain in the American Army and waiting for transportation home at the close of World War I. Dr. Colvin had been invited to discuss how this American decision to banish alcoholic drink had occurred—the moral, civic, and industrial factors that had influenced the decision by the United States and particularly the democratic processes by which it had come. His contacts were at the faculty level and among educational leaders in and outside of the university field. My commission in 1920 was to work with interested student organizations, teachers' colleges, and related agencies. There were at that time organized student abstinence societies and unorganized non-drinking groups, small but very vigorous, in the central and northern European universities and secondary schools. In Sweden, Norway, Denmark, Holland, Switzerland, Finland, Germany, Austria, and among the nations that later became Czechoslovakia and Yugoslavia they had headquarters of their own. They were carrying on educational programs in the lower schools as well as in their own colleges.

After conferences with leaders in England and the organizations in Holland, Switzerland, Sweden, and France, we were invited to attend the summer school of the Swedish Student Temperance Movement, SSUH, at Karlstadt, Sweden, an outstanding summer event that included not only students of Sweden but also groups from Norway, Denmark, and Finland. This conference had gained a reputation for its objective and scientific program and approach. It had been going on for years.

Difference in Approach

SSUH had been sponsoring this summer conference for forty years previous to 1920. It was a well organized and efficient student abstinence and educational movement. It had at that time local branches in all the universities, the gymnasiums, the technical schools, and many middle-schools throughout Sweden. In 1920, it was reported that the Sveriges Studerande Ungdoms Helnyketerhetsforbund had 4,893 members. To encourage personal abstinence, to change social customs and ideals that were free from the pressure of social drink, and to encourage the popularity and the joy of the non-drink life were their outstanding purposes.

The society conducted courses of systematic study of the scientific aspect of the question for students, the courses advancing from year to year. It gave, each year, a series of lectures in Stockholm for advanced students, teachers, and the public. Its qualified members visited hundreds of lower grade schools, aiding teachers and talking in classes. Text books, study outlines, and other literature were published. A well-illustrated magazine was issued semi-monthly from SSUH headquarters at Upsala University.

Karlstadt: and "Alcohol-Free Culture"

The summer conference of 1920 was attended by university students, who alone were permitted to wear the distinctive Swedish student cap, studying youth from the "colleges" or gymnasiums, cooperating faculty members, recent graduates, leaders in the public schools, and fraternal representatives from Norway, Denmark, Germany, and Finland. In them, we soon discovered an idealism based on objective scientific study of alcoholic drink culture that had not been understood or utilized in the temperance movements or the IPA in the United States. This ten-day educational approach at Karlstadt was a very realistic expression of the meaning and objectives of the Swedish student movement, an "Alco-hol-Frei Kulture".

It was also a school for equipping members of the SSUH to organize programs of study courses for lower grade schools and conduct them as visiting instructors. Hundreds did it every year. The lecturers at Karl-stadt were among the highest in scientific and educational standing in Scandinavia.

The outstanding feature of this summer school of "abstaining stu-dents", of 1920 was their "joyousness". They said, "We are always sing-ing." They greeted us with songs when we arrived at the railroad station and they continued every day of the conference.

To demonstrate the conviction that "the alcohol-free life is the hap-piest life," recreation, games, folk-dances and spontaneous singing packed every day with fun and fury. One day, the whole School—scientists, visitors, and all—were taken on a twelve hour tour that included the country home of Selma Lagerlif, world-noted Swedish writer.

Wakened at 4 A.M., Mrs. Warner and I, who had arrived from Switzerland late the night before with almost no sleep for two days, were served coffee and cakes by three students in a private home; guided to the train-station where a hundred students were circling and singing while waiting for the train. We boarded a third-class coach to a lake station, where we had coffee. On the lake steamer, a substantial breakfast followed, roast beef, gravy, and potatoes; a wonderful lake trip of several hours; off at a small station, we found waiting a long line of hay-rack wagons with plenty of hay; then, five or six miles through typical small towns and scenic country; after this, a half-mile march with banners and flags flying and never ending jest and chatter, we came to the country estate of the world popular novelist who had invited the group to visit her. A very formal but pleasing approach was made to this noted writer answered with warm greetings from the hostess; a tour of the premises; a reception in the large yard—with cookies and cherries; a deeply scientific lecture in the barn, the students sitting in fresh hay. Those of us who did not understand Swedish, a German student priest and I, explored the nearby woods. After another half-mile march to a recreation spot in the forest, we had a real picnic dinner. After two hours of lectures and brilliant Swedish folk dancing by competing groups from different provinces, we had another picnic from the leftovers; the return trip by hay-racks; another by lake steamer with (to be modern) a "snack" on board; the train to Karlstadt and a real smorgasbord in the formal but frisky re-greetings to the visitors, who had to learn the approach to this midnight dinner the hard way—leading off in parade of 150 joking students. It was a glorious "Alcohol-Frei" day.

When lecture hours came, these north-land students were serious and strictly scientific. The week gave opportunity for talks, leading toward the organization of an international movement that had been proposed at an earlier conference in London.

A committee representing SSUH, the IPA, and university leaders was appointed to call a conference of all student non-drinking groups in Europe and America to meet the following year at the International Congress on Alcoholism at Lausanne, Switzerland, to form an organization at the college and university level. I was asked to present the plan and extend an invitation in all the countries that I expected to visit during the following four months. These contacts included a British summer school at Port Rush, Ireland; a speaking tour among student groups in Holland and Switzerland; a conference at a Paris theological seminary; one with faculty members in the four universities of Belgium; a second conference tour in all the countries I had visited earlier and several of the colleges and universities in England, including seven at Oxford and three at Cambridge.

Was It a Kidnap?

Sincere interest as well as curiosity was keen—and very, very controversial—that year. The United Kingdom Alliance in London arranged my dates and had accepted an invitation from the organized student body at Sheffield University for an evening talk and questioning. On arrival, I was given a courtesy tour of the university buildings and campus. There were perhaps 125 students at the meeting. The presiding officer, president of the student body, made a friendly introduction. Then the lights went out. A half-dozen fellows seized the chairman and the speaker, took us down the stairs and into a waiting war-discarded Red Cross Ambulance, and five of us took a four or five mile ride. Lying under this form of British restriction, we had a lively discussion about freedom of speech and personal liberty. I suggested that we go back and debate it before the group. These fellows, mostly medical students, said "we don't want the freshmen to get (your) ideas about beer." In a suburb of Sheffield, we found the end of a trolley line that led to my hotel in the city. The next morning, a short article appeared in a city daily. I went back to the campus to let it be seen that freedom of speech had not been cut short by the invited American speaker.

Later in the year, a public debate was arranged at King College, Fleet Street, London, to honor William J. "Pussy-foot" Johnson, who the previous year had been kidnapped by a mixed crowd of hoodlums and students after his speaking date at that college. He had lost an eye by a stone thrown, but not by a student, that had resulted in blindness. The debate was an expression of friendship and loyalty to the principle of freedom of speech in honor of Mr. Johnson. There were four debators, two speakers against the principle of prohibition and an American and a British expert for it. My British colleague and I were the defense. The audience, students and university people discussed vigorously among themselves, then voted against what America had done, but in the really surprising majority of two to one.

Lausanne, 1921

Some of these countries, Norway, Yugoslavia, and others, had established temperance or abstinence organizations. In Denmark, the Students' Abstinence Society had 500 members in ten local societies, the biggest at the University of Copenhagen with 200 members. There was an abstinence group at the University of Helsinki, Finland, that had been active since 1886. Similar groups were active in other countries of Europe.

The conference initiated at the SSUH school in 1920 convened in Lausanne, Switzerland, August 27, 1921, with representatives from 31 student organizations in twelve countries. After three days of discussion, "The World Student Federation Against Alcoholism" was organized with the following officers: President, Dr. Courtney C. Weeks, London, Medical officer in the British Army during the war; Secretary, Onno van der Veene, University of Leiden, Holland; and International Secretary, Harry S. Warner, Chicago, Illinois, USA; Members of the Executive Committee, Sigfrid Borgstrom, Upsala University, Sweden; and Robert Joos, University of Zurich, Switzerland.

The federation adopted as its purpose: "To create, propagate, and deepen among the students in higher institutions of learning in all countries, the study of the causes, effects, and prevention of alcoholism." Member organizations in each nation had full freedom "to adjust this program to the needs of their own national life."

An International Committee, one member from each society, was founded to guide the work and elect the officers each two years. The IPA offered our periodical, *The Intercollegiate Statesman,* as the organ of the Federation and changed its name to *The International Student.* It was sent free to the officers of the national and local societies and, within three years, had correspondents in 21 countries.

It was in the atmosphere of 650 scientists, educators, official government delegates, medical and research specialists, social workers, and temperance leaders from around the world, attending the Fourteenth International Congress on Alcoholism, that students and university educators of Europe and America met in a group of their own in response to the call initiated at Karlstadt, Sweden, the previous year. It was a vision of what union of these groups in institutions of higher learning could mean in those years following the end of World War I that led to this partly spontaneous conference of students, professors, teachers, and delegates of student organizations from all the Central and Northern European countries, Great Britain, and the United States. They represented many viewpoints and wanted to find a common ground on which interested students of all countries could unite. This active minority of university students and students in all higher schools expressed a sense of responsibility that the rugged necessity that faced other classes had fallen to them.

Looking to A New Era

The vision of the founders of the World Student Federation was expressed by Dr. Weeks in his presidential address at Copenhagen in 1923, "The Threshold of a New Era".

> Especially do we ask those who are not abstainers to join in the systematic study of the various aspects of the (alcohol) problem. I make no apology for those who are abstainers. We are such, not because we do not like it (alcoholic drink), not because we wish to remove any legitimate pleasure from the life of our people, nor because we desire to sit in judgement on those who differ from us; but because we honestly and sincerely

> believe that alcoholism has been brought to the bar of human judgement and stands condemned in the fact that it militates against the welfare of society, the integrity of the home, and the highest realization of the human personality.

Drink compulsions in the universities were losing force in the 1920's. Young people of Great Britain were not flocking to the public house as had their fathers. "A striking feature in the revolt of modern youth against conventional customs and social habits inherited and adhered to for generations is their attitude to the alcohol tradition," wrote an English observer in 1931. "There is abundant evidence that young England knows that such statements as 'beer is best' will not bear examination. If proof of this change in thought and habit is needed, it can be seen in the great beer advertising campaign recently launched by the brewers, the director of which said, 'the chief customers of the public house today are the elderly and middle aged man.'"

In Germany, the youth movements regarded the beer mug as a symbol of an age that was passing. Expressing a passionate protest against materialism, artificiality, and old social customs, they emphasized natural living, recreation, and outdoor activities. One national group of a million or more were total abstainers; others were practically so. In 1926, the societies in the general council numbered 4,338,850 young people below 21 years of age. A new generation was growing up in Germany with an attitude toward drink traditions that contrasted dramatically with that of their fathers.

Similar youth movements were active from Norway to Yugoslavia. Student interest in alcoholic pleasure began to reflect the change. Serious questioning of drink had begun to differentiate this small but vigorous non-alcoholic culture. The millions in the youth movements of Europe, previous to the rise of totalitarianism, while mid-Europe was relatively democratic, were gradually discarding drink customs and replacing them with outdoor games, hikes, and folk dancing.

It was on my third tour of Central Europe, in 1923, that I saw something of these great "Youth Movements" with their millions of super-idealistic members in Germany. They had been rebelling against the drink customs of the past. Sharp antagonism and total abstinence was being expressed by some sections of this movement. The earnestness with which these youth faced the beer drinking customs and the wine and beer industries in the first post-war period was almost incredible. The key to the future in non-drinking culture in Middle Europe seemed to be in the hands of the "studying youth" just before Hitler's day.

I will never forget an afternoon in Hamburg, August 1928, when I saw 600 abstaining German youth marching in converging groups to a meeting of their own. I heard their shouts, saw their banners from my hotel, then joined and marched with them, and listened to their speaker, a noted German educator and a scientist. They were singing, happy to be free from the after war poverty. One fourth or more of the youth of Germany stood clear cut in their hope for a future alcohol-free culture.

Wanted From America—Reliable Information

The outstanding impression that one found on these tours was the eagerness for reliable reporting about how "the American experiment" was going and cooperation with American students and educators. Opinions from these sources they could understand. Their newspapers, magazines, and more serious reports were filled with propaganda. The law had been declared to be a failure before it was tried; it was taken by many as a joke. They wanted factual information which they could not readily obtain. In four conference visits, 1920, 1921, 1923, and 1927, contacting the representatives of ten countries, I caught much of the dedication that marked all the younger groups and leaders that were participating in all of the various non-drinking activities of the universities, middle schools, and the youth movements of the various countries.

CHAPTER IX

IDEALISM MEETS REALISM

IMMEDIATELY FOLLOWING THE National Convention of the IPA at Des Moines, Iowa, January 5, 1920, and our final National Oratorical Contest, the officers and field secretaries met in Washington, just as National Prohibition came into effect, to plan for the future by renewing emphasis on basic education. Such a program, it seemed certain, would be as necessary as before to meet the new and unknown problems in the college field, as well as the general public. It was believed, also, that educational programs would now be more effective under the policy of prohibition than had been possible under permission and license. Many in college communities as well as in the public expected quick, decisive results; but many more, perhaps the majority, while rejoicing that a dramatic and radical step had been taken, anticipated that a long period of struggle and education would be imperative.

Changes were made in the organization of the Association. Dr. D. Leigh Colvin, founder and President since 1899, with the exception of four years when Virgil G. Hinshaw held that position, resigned to give his time and support to the political field and to write a history of the Prohibition Party.[1] Daniel A. Poling, Vice-President for years, was elected President. Harry S. Warner, General Secretary since 1900, resigned in favor of a younger man and became Educational Secretary, later International Secretary.

Representatives of the major temperance agencies and several church denominations were added for the first time to an enlarged Board of Directors. Hitherto, control of the Association had been in the hands of those who organized it and students from the succeeding academic generations following 1900. It was hoped that larger financial support could thus be obtained for the enlarged program that all recognized as inevitable for the immediate future if banishment of commercialized liquor and the saloon was to be completed. The Intercollegiate Associa-

---

1. A year later, July, 1920, Dr. Colvin was the candidate of the Prohibition Party for Vice-President of the United States.

tion thus became the agency, for a short period, of various movements for service in the college field. At the same time, it lost some of the independent status it had gained between 1900 and 1920.

The Amendment marked the beginning of a new era in which this "adventure in freedom" from the domination of alcohol could steadily be brought about by creative measures that would be more fundamental than legal control, regulation, or even the principle of prohibition itself.

Thus, the victorious idealism of 1920 flowered into a vision of the future, but with a realistic forecast of the educational work that had yet to be done to free the nation from drunkenness. Anticipating the reaction that was bound to come, notwithstanding the century of struggle for temperance, and the half-century of prohibition experiments at the local and state levels, it was fully expected by those who had shared these experiences that a growth in law violation and difficulty of enforcement would involve the present and many later generations of students. Dr. Daniel A. Poling, newly elected President, in his address of the year, brought a creative challenge, as he had often done at previous crises, through the Association to the colleges of America when he said:

> The battle lines that are forming now in the world war against beverage alcohol invite with distinct challenge the men and women of American colleges and universities. . . . I have watched the world go by, counting her woes and crying her needs. I have weighed well the claims of other causes. It is my conviction that nowhere else in the whole program of social progress does a man or a woman find a finer struggle and a braver fight.

This was the period in which the ideal of a League of Nations was dominant in world attention. It was the ideal of President Woodrow Wilson and more than half of the American public, for which the President gave his life. Although it failed in World War I years, it became a reality later—the present United Nations.

The meaning of the *Prohibition Movement,* as it came to me personally before and following the adoption of this policy of dealing with the problem of alcoholic drink, was expressed in an editorial at the time as follows: "It was never believed by thinking men that the Eighteenth or any other amendment would bring sudden transformation to American life. Only the non-thinking part of the public expected that or 'fell for' the idea that 'it's all over' when the Amendment was ratified."

The experienced leaders of the larger organizations, the colleges, and the churches in general who had shared in bringing national prohibition well knew that:

> . . . to free a society of 110,000,000 people with inherited customs drawn from all nationalities on earth, from the whole institution of alcoholic drink—its social traditions of 5,000 years, its physical desire and craving, its tremendous source of economic gain, its capacity for political intrigue —would require a far deeper and longer process than could be accomplished by law. "Whether this takes five years, or ten years, or a generation," many of them said, "it must continue to be the final aim."[2]

Uniting World "Alcohol-Free" Activities

Early in 1922, the Intercollegiate Association was invited to have a part in the first convention of the World League Against Alcoholism at Toronto, Canada. This new cooperative movement had just been organized to unite the anti-alcohol agencies of many countries for a post-war advance against alcoholism.

Held for six days in November, the convention was a world event. It registered over 1,100 delegates representing 45 national organizations with widely varying views.

Organized June 7, 1919, by Dr. Ernest H. Cherrington of the United States, Dr. Robert Hercod of Switzerland, and Rev. Ben H. Spence of Canada, and with strong cooperation from British scientists and temperance leaders, this outstanding event reflected the vision, the spirit, and the actual work going on in many countries in the post-World War I period. It had been inspired largely by the recent success of the anti-alcohol movements, war-time, constitutional, and legislative measures that had grown strong in North America, Canada as well as the United States.

The World League Against Alcoholism reflected a *decidedly new approach* and understanding of the human disorders latent in the consumption of alcoholic beverages. Its purpose was realistic, one on which many groups could unite. Stated in the constitution, it read: ". . . to attain by means of education and legislation the total suppression throughout the world of alcoholism . . . produced by the consumption of alcoholic beverages."

As a part of this world convention, the Intercollegiate Association organized a conference of students from foreign countries who were attending universities and colleges in North America. Thirty-six different

2. Ernest H. Cherrington, *The Evolution of Prohibition in the United States*, p. 370.

nations, largely Spanish American, were represented. The theme was ". . . to consider the place in which the world struggle against alcohol, now centering in North America, would soon occupy in the life and thinking of students the world around."

College students occupied one main session of the convention; they were regular delegates. They shared its activities and caught the spirit and vision of this new world-wide movement that had brought together noted speakers, scientists, research experts, writers, and 1,100 leaders from sixty-six different countries.

Dr. Ira Landrith, who had succeeded Dr. Daniel A. Poling as President of the IPA, gave the keynote address—an enthusiastic look to the future of cooperation among college and university students in other countries. Dr. August Ley, University of Brussels, reported a very recent interest in the universities of Belgium and other French-speaking countries. Dr. J. G. Hume, University of Toronto, spoke for Canada and Rev. Elmer L. Williams of Chicago, appealed to the students of North America "to take part in the big game of law enforcement and the creation of higher civic ideals among the influential classes" of the United States and Canada. Both countries at that time had full or limited degrees of legal prohibition. Harry S. Warner, Secretary of the Association, spoke on "The Student Field at Home and Abroad", reporting on his eight months of group committees and personal conferences among the universities and colleges in Europe the previous year as seen after his 22 years among American colleges.

Dr. Ernest H. Cherrington, General Secretary and founder of the World League, forecast the opportunities open to the men and women, "now in college, for definite, personal service throughout the world."

There was particularly large attendance of Spanish American students at this World Convention. They took steps toward bringing the new movement for the prevention of alcoholism to the attention of the universities and higher schools from which they had come. The nations represented by students in the convention, in addition to Canada and the United States, were Albania, Argentina, Armenia, Brazil, British East Africa, Bulgaria, Burma, Colombia, Czechoslovakia, Dominican Republic, Borneo, Georgia, Great Britain, Hindustan, Hungary, India, Ireland, Italy, Jugoslavia, Liberia, Lithuania, Macedonia, Mexico, Peru, Puerto Rico, Romania, Russia, Siam, Siberia, Sierra Leone, South Africa, Turkey, Ukrainia, Venezuela, and Wales.

The Toronto World Convention, as it appeared to me then and as I write more than forty years later, "lifted the whole conception of the movement from that of saving the victim to that of removing one of the most perplexing and destructive forces in the economic and social life of modern nations."

There were four messages that forecast strength of the deeper understanding of the world problem of alcohol that had already come to the front and on which the new advance to reduce and ultimately eliminate alcoholism had already begun to act: (a) the increasing attention relating to health and general welfare of the individual, the race, and the community; (b) the international commercial and industrial developments at the end of World War I; (c) the relation between drink and labor; (d) and the results of the removal of liquor by law and continued support of the law by public opinion.

The addresses that carried new basic thinking were those by Dr. C. W. Salebee, Chairman of the British National Birth-Rate Commission: "The Opportunity and Obligations of the World League Against Alcoholism" by Dr. Ernest H. Cherrington; "Organized Labor and Prohibition" by John G. Cooper of the American Federation of Labor, a United States Congressman; "Prohibition in the Province of Ontario" and its relation to government, local, national, and international by E. C. Drury, Prime Minister of Ontario, Canada, where the law as a war measure was regarded as a reasonable success. Nearly fifty speakers and writers participated in this tremendous six-day exchange of ideas, scientific research, experience and look to the future.

Anti-Pros Organize Internationally

"Toronto, 1922", answered a challenge that had come a month earlier from an Anti-Prohibition minded convention in Brussels, Belgium, attended by delegates from all European and many American countries—including both anti-prohibition leaders and businessmen seeking to preserve their sources of liquor profits. This Brussels convention launched a program to check the advance of the non-drinking movements of all lands, raised a large fund, established world headquarters in Paris, and announced their intention to carry the campaign into the United States and all countries that were seeking to free themselves from alcohol by legal restraint or banishment.

This Brussels convention of 1922 brought together many educators and scientists as well as the "wets" of the world, into growing unity.

To the reformers, the Toronto Convention revealed the growing strength in public opinion toward reducing the consumption of alcoholic drink that had come to have world-wide beginnings at that time; in growing scientific knowledge, economic public costs, and realism; in capable leadership, devotion, and zeal, that if wisely coordinated might be expected to move forward until the age-old corruption in everyday human living due to alcohol could be greatly reduced in human society.

Soon after the Toronto Convention, the Intercollegiate Association joined the World League Against Alcoholism and became the College Department of that new coordinating agency. Headquarters were moved from Chicago to Washington in May, 1923. Enlarged financial aid was received and unlimited freedom granted to carry on the educational policies and programs of previous years and to organize in any country where cooperation could be found or created at the higher education level, looking to the equipment of leaders for future service. Within three years, Robert H. Rolofson, a former field secretary, was elected Executive Secretary and I became International Educational Secretary for the second time.

Idealism Meets Realism

To the reformers in the United States, who for a century and a half had been seeking to reduce drunkenness by reducing the production and sale of alcoholic liquors and enlarging the area of non-drinking culture, a supreme test had come by the mid-twenties.

The legal saloon had gone; the liquor-producing industry was delegalized; the frontier grog shop had disappeared; prestige drinking customs were less influential; high society pressure was less inclusive; and the legalized saloon keeper was "put out of business". No longer could the saloon keeper point to the license back of his bar as proof of his good citizenship and observance of law—of his right to sell repeated drinks to men who were becoming intoxicated and adding danger to others as they had been doing after "just one more".

No longer could "the law" or the judge rule as often on the side of the lawbreaker who had supplied this anesthetic drug for a half-century with little control to practically all who applied. A situation had arrived when social welfare movements, religious influence, and non-propagandistic education would have a chance to function freely with the aid of the law.

"After an examination of all the data I have estimated that the flow of alcohol down human throats in the United States is at present less than 16%, probably less than 5% of pre-prohibition consumption," wrote Professor Irving Fisher in 1926 in *Prohibition at Its Worst.*

These convictions were widely prevalent in the opinion of the "drys" of that period. A constructive step had been taken. Now there could be fair competition between the conflicting concepts regarding the use and the non-use of alcohol as a popular beverage.

But after the first five years, most supporters of prohibition "became acutely aware that the battle had only been half won . . . that a struggle for proper enforcement would have to be as realistic and uncompromising as that for its adoption."

Exploiting Student Disorders

During those thirteen years and long before and ever since, certain types of newspapers and magazines have greedily seized upon the disorders of college students, exaggerated the incidents and exploited them beyond all reason. Naturally, the publications of the alcohol industry did the same. *The American Brewer,* January 1, 1928, said: "Twenty-one bootleggers, including a deputy sheriff and a woman, were arrested by prohibition agents, December 15, on the campus of the University of Alabama."

"Eight college students were dismissed from Syracuse University for drinking liquor prior to a football game, according to the *Syracuse Herald.*"

"Eleven students at the Taft School, Watertown, Conn., for being intoxicated at a dance in the school gym, were arrested on Thanksgiving night."

There were thousands of similar news stories in 1925 in the daily newspapers and magazines before, during, and following the thirteen experimental "dry" years; some true, some containing a trace of fact grossly exaggerated from minor incidents; others wholly fabricated and written in sensational style.

The first five years following the adoption of national prohibition showed highly favorable data in many aspects of our social history. The legislatures of the states which had not adopted state prohibition earlier now enacted enforcement codes, with the exception of Maryland, which already had similar laws by counties.

Organizing for Repeal

But in the heavily populated states and the big cities where the idea of limiting or removing the sale of alcohol by local option or local vote, and in the states where the test had occurred only in rural and small city communities, the legislatures began to repeal existing enforcement measures and to leave the main problem of enforcement to the Federal government. This placed a double burden on the Federal commissioners and deprived them of the cooperation intended by the Constitutional provision for joint enforcement. Federal agents and courts in these areas became heavily overburdened.

Taking advantage of this situation in the cities, the Association Against the Prohibition Amendment, organized before the law came into effect, began many heavy drives for repeal. It organized businessmen's committees, women's groups, lawyers, artists, writers, doctors, and others in every state. It became active, aggressive, in politics, seeking particularly to defeat legislators and congressmen who had supported the Eighteenth Amendment. It fought to dominate both the major political parties and their nominating conventions.

The Normal Opposition: (1) Cultural Backgrounds

During this same five years, the most successful period of the thirteen years, resistance to the national policy began and grew stronger from four different angles of approach.

First, there was the little changed "Natural Opposition", the tradition and culture of those who had long depended upon "drink" as necessary, in spite of its tendency to end in intoxication. The satisfactions they gained were deeply embedded in their traditions and culture. To the millions who felt that alcohol was a necessity in their daily lives, prohibition was a calamity. Many began to make it for themselves and, so long as this was within their private lives, in the home, it had not been forbidden, although they could not sell it. Others, particularly many with large incomes or wealth, were indifferent to their responsibility as citizens and began to defy the law or found ways of evading it. In order to avoid being without a good supply in their cellars, particularly in the first few years, many of the top social classes had done as Upton Sinclair vividly illustrated:

> Uncle Bland recognized the oncoming Prohibition before the legislation actually became part of our Constitution in 1918. He laid in a good supply of wines, whiskies, brandies, and liquors in the cellar of his Catonsville Mansion—only the best brands and vintages for John Randolph Bland, and they cost him six thousand dollars in all. . . . Thieves entered, carried off every case of his treasure.[3]

True, there had been a long-time and generally accepted philosophy

3. Upton Sinclair, *The Cup of Fury,* p. 73.

of moderation and self-control. This had been the basis of some temperance movements in all Western nations for two previous centuries. To millions, "temperance" meant temperance, not "abstinence". But when the reform groups of America and Great Britain included "total abstinence" as the outstanding meaning of the word "temperance", others in the general public continued to use it in its original meaning as "moderate" use. This double use of the word has been a confusing fact for a hundred years in the struggles to reduce drunkenness or enlarge the non-drinking culture of America. Both conceptions continue to occupy positions of influence in public thinking and in the formation of attitudes ever since.

The long-time moderation approach of "temperance" in its original meaning might have helped more to solve the alcohol problem had its supporters recognized earlier the basic cultural sources of the drinking problem as a whole. The double meaning of the word "temperance" continued long into the period when the outstanding purpose of the positive reformers was to reduce the sources and cultural patterns of the consumption of alcoholic beverages in society. This confusion was deeper than the friends of reform could understand at that time. The Eighteenth Amendment brought these two ways of thinking to a critical head. Had the friends of moderation been alert half a century earlier, while the philosophy and practice of legal prohibition were growing strong from vast experience into what seemed to be a practical necessity, this confusion to them in 1920 and after would have seemed less sudden or drastic. As the Sociologist Ross defined the acute issue:

> Far, then, from being a gratuitous stroke at a dying custom, prohibition was an urgent social-defense measure forced by greedy liquor interests which were so short sighted that they would not leave non-drinkers alone. Continually, they plotted to tempt the public into a larger consumption. Their ambition seemed to be to convert the rising generation of males into peripatetic tanks.[4]

The Natural Opposition: (2) Economic Interests

The assumption that one has the right to make a living and earn profits was inherent to the resistance of many seriously questionable industries, as well as the sale of beverage alcohol was inherent to traffic. To the liquor industry, it had begun to be a life or death struggle. The defeat it had suffered when Congress submitted and the states adopted the Amendment was heavy.

---

4. Edward A. Ross, "As the Sociologist Sees It", *Intercollegiate Statesman,* October, 1921.

As an indication of what the future would bring, a survey study made in 1921 stated: "Just before July 1, 1917, when war-time prohibition put the ban on the liquor traffic in the United States, there were in operation 177,790 retail alcohol establishments, 669 breweries and distilleries. Many of those were transformed into other industries during the year in anticipation of prohibition. Of the 236 distilleries in operation on July 1, 1918, one year before the beginning of the war-time prohibition regime, 162 of them adjusted to the new order."[5]

One illustration of what happened to distilling plants was found in the world's greatest whiskey center, Peoria, Illinois, where 13 former distilleries were taken over by a large food corporation. They formerly employed about 1,000 men in the manufacture of alcohol. After the take-over, more than 4,000 were employed and manufactured thirty different products: industrial alcohol, stock food, wheat flour, cane syrup, corn oils, yeast, preserves, jellies, jams, and vinegar.

The following list taken at random suggests the economic improvement and increase in employment that ensued: Several brewing buildings of Cincinnati, Ohio, were converted into what has grown to be the largest clothing manufacturing establishment in the world. The Chicago Brewery of the United Breweries was sold at a handsome price to a stove manufacturing company. The Southern Brewery of Boston became a candy factory as did the Liberty Brewery of Pittsburgh. The National Capital Brewery at Washington, employing 50 people and using $130,000 worth of raw materials a year became an ice cream factory employing 150 people and using $400,000 worth of raw materials yearly. A brewery of Rochester, New York, became a crude oil refinery. The Mt. Hood Brewery of Portland, Oregon, was used for the smoking and curing of fish. Former saloon sites by the hundreds were turned into candy shops, ice cream parlors, soda fountains, restaurants, clothing stores, drug stores, cafeterias, cigar stands, meat shops, and other retail merchandise establishments.

As a natural sequence, therefore, Irving Fisher, Yale economist, had substantial foundation for his estimate in 1926 when he said: "After an examination of all the data I have estimated that the flow of alcohol down human throats in the United States is at present certainly less than 16%, probably less than 5% of pre-prohibition consumption."[6]

---

5. Ernest H. Cherrington, *What Became of The Breweries, Distilleries and Saloons?*
6. Irving Fisher, *International Student,* November, 1923.

(3) Resistance-Created Propaganda

As evidence pointed toward the beginnings of success in the prohibition policy, in spite of terrific evasion and violation of the laws, there began to appear after the first five years a high-level resistance to the amendment which became more aggressive. The directing agency was the Association Against the Prohibition Amendment. The goal of the AAPA was frankly stated: (1) "To prevent the country from going on a bone-dry (First World War) basis." (2) "To make the Eighteenth Amendment forever inoperative."[7]

Thus, from its conception, this organization had visioned not only ultimate repeal, but also nullification as a measure that would encourage lawlessness and finally defiance, should the ordinary methods of changing public opinion fail to meet their objectives.

Looking toward a new period of activity, the AAPA organized women's clubs, businessmen's committees, and others widely throughout the country; lobbyists from AAPA persistently sought to modify enforcement, interpret regulations, turn enforcement back to the states, to declare wine and beer non-intoxicating and to obstruct enforcement.[8]

The stability of the 18th Amendment and the law founded on it would thus be undermined. Many successive measures to this end were later declared unconstitutional by the courts.

As seen by Irving Fisher and other economists, it was the people who wanted to sell "drink" rather than those who wanted to drink "drink" who were the major force that brought about repeal before the policy could be adequately tested.[9] Many sociologists, economists, and educators—far beyond the pressure of the "reformers"—agreed with Fisher and his associates. More time, they said at that time, was necessary to give so great a national welfare movement a satisfactory test. For the tests of the first five to seven years had been far more meaningful than was anticipated or even dreamed possible by many substantial leaders of the "cause"—all that could be expected in so short a period was the opinion of most thinking people. One historical writer said, "the early years immediately following the adoption of National Prohibition showed the most favorable data in our national history." This was not all due, of course, to this one cause, for the period was one of general prosperity.

---

7. Fletcher Dobyns, *The Amazing Story of Repeal,* p. 326.
8. *Ibid.*
9. Irving Fisher, *Prohibition at Its Worst.*

After 1925, resistance built up rapidly. Law violation became "big business". The lure of illegal profits gained in widely scattered areas, law violators organized themselves into gangs of bootleggers to defeat the law, and highjacked each others night running rival trucks. There was rum-running from the Kentucky-Tennessee mountains, the city slum stills, the Canadian border, and the offshore ships from various countries "parked off the Atlantic coast waiting for the midnight motor boats from the shore."

After 1925, the AAPA and similar agencies came out aggressively in their propaganda for repeal. The president, Pierre S. DuPont, an outstanding businessman of the DuPont Industries of Delaware, had supported prohibition a few years earlier. Continuing non-drink rules to thousands of their employees, he and his associates proposed a tax on liquor so heavy that it could be a substitute for much of the Federal Income tax. Such a tax, he failed to consider, would vastly increase the market for bootlegging, already the heaviest obstacle to the enforcement of the law. It would also greatly reduce the personal and company taxes of the DuPonts and associates by millions of dollars.[10]

The saloon, re-named "tavern", had been "the most effective agency for promoting the sale of liquor that had ever been devised." That objective had not appeared as openly in the first five years of the prohibition period.

Opposition Threatens Nullification

As explained by Dobyns:

> When the representatives of big business reached the conclusion that it would be profitable to bring the liquor traffic back and tax it, they withdrew their active and passive support from prohibition, allied themselves with the liquor interests, the underworld, and every other reactionary and subversive element, and threw the entire weight of their wealth and power into the battle for repeal. Their first move was to defeat and destroy all politicians everywhere who stood for retention and enforcement of prohibition, and to supplant them with pliant tools who would permit liquor lawlessness, act as sounding boards for wet propaganda, and work and vote for repeal.

One severe handicap in the first few years was that the responsibility for enforcement of the prohibition laws remained under the Department of the Treasury. Andrew Mellon, a great treasurer, was the owner of

---

10. Dobyns, *op. cit.*

millions of distillery and other liquor property. It was too much to expect of political human nature that administration of this law, under these circumstances, would be very effective. After the removal of the prohibition unit to the Department of Justice and the placing of enforcement officers under Civil Service instead of political appointment, the reports of success from Federal agents were decidedly better.

Then came repeal of the Eighteenth Amendment, in 1932, and return of control of beverage alcohol to the states by the Twenty-first Amendment, just as the brewing industry had come to acknowledge that "half the expected market for beer does not exist today."

> "When beer comes back," an advertisement prepared for *The Brewing Industry,* November 19, 1932, for distribution among college student newspapers, asked: "What are the first steps brewers will take to restore temperate drinking among the youth of the land? Obviously, there must be a campaign of education and the one field in which this can be conducted is, fortunately, the most important of all for immediate and future business—the colleges. . . . Not one tenth of one percent of the youth in college know what really good beer tastes like.

Chapter X

BACKGROUND HISTORY OF THE EARLIER PERIOD

WHILE WRITING THIS HEADLINE, a consulting psychologist across the hall from my office brought to my desk a new transistor radio, pocket-size, that stirred our mutual admiration. It was so modern.

Neither youthful idealism nor scientific research could imagine such a discovery a half-century ago. But the "inventions" made in a century of political and social experimentation toward reducing alcoholic excesses and alcoholism in everyday living have produced no such dramatic results. There has been real advance in periods of deep concern and substantial efforts to reform, but followed by periods of recession and some re-study of the problem in the light of deepening knowledge and the road-blocks discovered by experience.

On January 16, 1919, the day that the thirty-sixth state ratified the Eighteenth Amendment of the Constitution, thereby de-legalizing and seeking to ban the manufacture and sale of intoxicating beverages in the United States of America, a New York newsman wrote:

> The country has never witnessed a political phenomenon as strange as the swift, uninterrupted progress of the prohibition amendment toward final passage. It is as if a sailing ship on a windless ocean was sweeping ahead, propelled by some invisible force. Perhaps our legislators are right and there is a strong, unseen current to account for the phenomenon.[1]

Both the legislators and the newswriters were right. There had been a current flowing steadily stronger and becoming more popular for nearly a century. Not fully seen perhaps by those reporters who had been persistently playing down for years the meaning of the thousands of local, county, and state campaigns to vote out local saloons and curb the liquor traffic, they did not appreciate the strength of the growing movement as a whole to reduce drunkenness. Seventeen states had adopted prohibition; others were in the midst of doing so. A heavy majority of the members in Congress had been chosen in election cam-

1. *The New York Times,* January 16, 1919.

paigns in which prohibition was a decisive issue. The main question had been debated over and over again, long before the Eighteenth Amendment came up for final action by Congress and was sent to the states for ratification.

State action came swiftly by the largest vote of states ever given to an amendment to the Federal Constitution—45 out of 48. This majority was equaled only by the vote on the 19th Amendment that gave women the right to vote. The 15th, or Anti-slavery Amendment, had been ratified by 33 of the 36 states and the Equal Rights by 30 of the 37. From this point of measurement, it was the most popular amendment ever adopted—the result of a steady trend for action at the national level that had been growing for a half-century.

The Columbia University historian, John Allen Krout, wrote in 1925:

> The Eighteenth Amendment was long on its way. Its ratification was not the result of temporary conditions taken at their flood, but the final expression of a fundamental change which had been more than a century in the making.[2]

Whatever else may be said in criticism or favor of the Prohibition reform down to 1919, it cannot be called sudden or unexpected. The forces that brought it about—religious, social, economic, political, and educational—had been active in every part of the country and at every level in society, except in the colonies of recent immigrants who had settled in great cities and mining communities, and at the opposite end of the social scale in limited groups of the socially elite.

Beginnings of Temperance and Moderation

In 1808, when the first temperance society was formed, almost everybody "took a little something" occasionally or oftener. Liquor was on the side-board, a table beverage in many families, a mark of hospitality when visitors called. Gentlemen caroused openly in the taverns. College commencements were sometimes an occasion for drinking together by students and teachers. Weddings, christenings, and funerals were incomplete without it. The clergy took it to inspire their sermons, the church accepted its moderate use. Society, more widely even than today, accepted "the cocktail hour" or its equivalent. Whiskey and brandy were recommended by the doctor and, in his absence, were the family cures of the pioneers. It was respectable, not merely to drink, but to get "gloriously drunk".

2. John Allen Krout, *The Origins of Prohibition,* p. 297.

Although so many drank, occasionally or regularly, the average consumption by each user was less than in later years. There were long periods when they could not obtain a supply. There were many long periods in the lives of most people when they were abstinent. Communities were not saturated with excessive advertising. There was no organized liquor industry to influence legislation.

Alcoholic liquors were sold in stores and taverns and manufactured by many small stills, not by great modern distillery companies. No scientific research had been given to the causes of alcoholism and drunkenness. But a steady change began after 1800 led by medical men, largely as health measures. Religious leaders and doctors began to repudiate immoderate drinking. Temperance societies spread everywhere over the country. A non-drinking class emerged that grew rapidly from year to year. A substantial section of society began to question the value of all drink customs and the presence of the tavern or saloon as a source of intolerable burdens and alcoholism. At first, they promoted "moderation", then "temperance", then abstinence, first from distilled liquors, then, after much experience from wine and beer as well. Every year hundreds of thousands pledged to quit or not to begin drinking.

Temperance Becomes Abstinence

One of the first temperance societies, at Moreau Springs, New York, in 1807, was started by a doctor, a farmer, and a barkeeper. They pledged themselves as a friendly group to abstain from "hard liquors". The penalty for breaking the pledge was a fine of 25 cents, later raised to 50 cents. Clubs were organized widely. It was then discovered that so "drastic" a pledge produced no lasting results.

Another pledge placed limitations on the frequency and the amount that could be taken at one time. After experience, it came to require abstinence. At first, it related to distilled liquors alone; later, to wines and beer, then called "temperance" drinks. The pledge then became "total abstinence" and signers assumed some obligation to win others to a non-drinking life.

There followed in the next thirty or forty years, a great variety of limited total abstinence and temperance movements that spread throughout North America, founding thousands of local organizations, increasing social and legal restrictions, and gaining church and public support.

Every year, there were great "temperance" crusades. One of the most dramatic was led by Father Matthew, a brilliant Catholic priest who came from Ireland in 1839 in answer to invitation, after having phenomenal success in his own country and in England. He promoted the pledge of complete abstinence. His reputation had become so international that he was met at the pier in New York by Congressmen. He was introduced at the White House and received by churches of all denominations. His two-year crusade over the United States yielded 800,000 abstinence pledges.

Similar crusades occurred continuously for nearly a century. John B. Gough, a reformed excessive drinker, or alcoholic, and a brilliant speaker, gave 8,600 addresses for the cause. John B. Finch, Francis Murphy, and many other emotional speakers were noted as temperance campaigners. A movement, The Washingtonians, became historic and spread widely because it was composed of heavy drinkers. It was organized by a group of tipplers in a tavern in Baltimore in April, 1840. It was similar in many ways to the Alcoholics Anonymous of a century later. But it was very different in that it cultivated publicity instead of anonimity and promoted campaigns which the A.A.'s of today carefully avoid.

Crusades by reformed drunkards, "rehabilitated Alcoholics" as they are called today, and temperance revivalists had been increasing the number of "tee-totalers" and moderate drinkers, and continued these activities down through 1900 and the following fifteen years of local option and state drives for Prohibition. Those whose names stand out with nation-wide prominence after 1900, included Dan Morgan Smith, Sam Small, and John G. Woolley. Towns, cities, and rural communities were reached repeatedly. Hundreds of thousands of men signed the pledge as a result of the personal experience of these reformed drinkers.

Growing Dependence on Law

From early in the century the appeal had been directed chiefly to frequent and excessive drinkers; later, it included moderate drinkers. Then, to prevent the beginning of the drinking habit and to influence others, the movements began to emphasize the total abstinence pledge as a basic movement in the reform.

When it was found that pledge signing and temperance agitation did not bring lasting results, the attractions of the public house and the profit interest of the drink seller became objects of attack.

It was seen that in spite of all that moderation and abstinence movements could do, the struggles of heavy drinkers to remain abstinent, of moderate drinkers to be moderate, of social drinkers to resist excess, at the very time that a general switch-over from the heavy pioneer use of "hard" liquors to beer was taking place, drunkenness and the consumption of alcohol continued. The liquor producing industries began to organize to resist taxation, then became powerful in politics. Advertising by industry became aggressive. The increasing per capita consumption substantiated these trends, and the pressures in society and on public affairs became a gigantic national problem.

Out of this complex situation the idea of prohibition by law became the most hopeful method of reducing the supply at the taverns and saloons. Steadily, through fifty years of rough experience, the emphasis changed from lifting the fallen to preventing the fall—from the tippler to the influences that led him to tipple and made it difficult for reclaimed drinkers to remain sober. There seems to have been a feeling of frustration among leaders of the temperance movement of that period, as they saw the limited results of their struggles for sobriety by pledge signing, moderation, moral persuasion, and the fellowship of abstinent groups of Good Templars. The drinkers who had been redeemed slipped back so often. Drastic procedures seemed to have become necessary.

Early Prohibition Experimenting

Then came the outstanding "temperance" event of the 19th century: The state of Maine adopted Constitutional Prohibition, June, 1851, under the lead of Neil Dow, a businessman of Portland. This act made American and world history. John Allen Krout wrote of it as a new approach or change of emphasis:

> It bore witness to the fact that the reformers had finally been forced to accept prohibition as a solution of the liquor problem. They had moral suasion for a half century and had found it wanting. The enactment of the Maine law marked the end of an epoch in temperance reform. Henceforth, the battle was to be waged not by precept and example, but by action.[3]

Actually, all the philosophies and most of the organizations that had been seeking solution continued in service. Most of them accepted the new policy at once. Those who rejected this technique asserted that moderation was true temperance. They criticized abstinence as tending toward prohibition.

Within six years, eleven states followed the example of Maine, before the Civil War in 1861. During the war, attention centered in the life-or-death of the Union; the public lost interest in the temperance movement. At the close of the war, Maine remained the one "dry" state.

3. *Ibid.*

Drinking was heavier and the liquor interests had become strongly organized and political minded by accepting federal taxation.

The Civil War blighted the temperance reform. Previous to its beginning, a dozen states had expressed themselves for prohibition of the "traffic".

As the country returned to normal living, after 1865, a new wave of pledge signing, increasing restrictions, and various forms of prohibition, local and state, swept over the country. The movement as a whole and particularly the resort to legal activities became more popular and aggressive. By the opening of the twentieth century, there were three dry states: Maine, Kansas, and North Dakota. There were also thousands of towns, counties, and city precincts that forbade the sale of intoxicants.

The conception was spreading that freedom from the drink tradition was the normal way of life, even while the per capita consumption was increasing. The prohibition movement was understood to be a step toward this conception rather than one toward the limitation of personal liberty. This in brief is an outline of the anti-liquor movement in the political field in 1900.

Diverging Trends Continue to Diverge

By the beginning of the twentieth century, there were two very different and outstanding cultural patterns side-by-side throughout North America and Western Europe. Both were growing. Both had deep roots in the mores and traditions of past ages; both were continuing to establish customs of their own and give them more active support. The non-drinking culture was in the minority, but vigorously active and growing rapidly. Viewed historically, however, it was not as deeply rooted as it should have been to support the rapid spread of the legal prohibitions that followed in the first quarter of the twentieth century as later events have shown.

At the very time of the tremendous sweep of legal restriction by local option, industrial restrictions and state prohibition, the consumption of liquor and the power of the liquor traffic had grown to a peak in political and economic power in public affairs. The situation was described in the conservative *Chicago Tribune,* July 17, 1910, as follows:

> If the secret records of the brewing and distilling industries were ever brought to light, they would tell a story of social and political corruption unequaled in the annals of our history. If the veritable narrative of the American saloon were ever written, it would make the decadence of Rome look like an age of pristine purity, in comparison.

Consequently, at the beginning of the century, the alcohol problem, as such, seemed to many realistic idealists, who were trying most seriously to do something, to be a question of legalizing or not legalizing the sale of alcohol for beverage purposes. There was a strong and very sincere belief that without license and legal approval, the sale of liquor could be controlled, as was and is the sale of other dangerous or questionable drugs. Beverage alcohol was called by some keen thinkers "The Legalized Outlaw". The license system, therefore, stood out as the place where change could first be made.

To refuse to license would, thus, deprive the saloon of its legal defense —make it an outlaw to be gradually eliminated as a nuisance; profit motives would be reduced; public disapproval increased; education and moral efforts could then be effective; the economic and political powers and the privileges of the industry undermined. The traffic in intoxicating liquors would then be de-legalized as slavery had been de-legalized. Public opinion then, including that of moderate users, would freely complete the change in customs by education and the sense of community responsibility.

More marked in the United States and Canada, the English-speaking and Scandinavian countries, than elsewhere, the non-drinking culture was growing under religious influence, education, and public experience of the consequences of alcoholic drink. Alcohol in various forms of educational propaganda had become a positive force in these nations.

Thus, the ideas of heavy restriction and prohibition became the outstanding goal of those who were seeking to remove the well-known dangers of drunkenness in everyday living. It had become a basic philosophy, a principle, because of the inherent intoxicating character of alcohol.

The drive for local "dry territory" by county, township, city, and state by state, increased until it merged with the drive toward an amendment to the Constitution. These continuous campaigns at the local level kept the problem close to the voters and enabled them to change their opinions from one election to another out of the experience they gained each few years. Stabilized public opinion thus grew out of repeated observations of the results of the prohibition idea.

If the saloon and the industry back of it could be removed, the backbone of the problem would be broken; after that, educational methods, and the demands of public safety and moral welfare would have a chance to reduce and perhaps eliminate the tragedy of drunkenness.

Throughout the years, the word "temperance" had stood out as a designation of the general movement but with differing ideologies back of it. To some sections of the public, it meant "restrained use", "moderate use", to others, "no use at all". With that section of society that was most earnestly seeking reform, it became synonymous with "total abstinence". Wherever drinking customs dominated, it suggested moderate use. The word had been a first step in the educational, political, and social programs of nearly all of those who were seeking to improve the situation. But its use after 1900 was often confusing; both pros and cons of reform claimed it as expressing their purpose.

Experience Yields Deeper Understanding

After the nineteenth century, pledge signing, concern for the children and wife of the heavy drinker, local and state restrictions on sale and production became the chief channels through which sobriety could be expected. The programs of "moral suasion" had yielded helpful, but short and limited improvements. Experience was interpreted as calling persistently for programs that would reach deeper sources. Slowly, steadily, through fifty years of hard-fought moral battles to save the drunkard, the emphasis changed from lifting the fallen to preventing the fall. A license was frequently refused by judges or defeated in local plebiscites; a long struggle between "wets" and "drys" over territory was in full swing. Social drink customs were being questioned more seriously by a growing part of society. But, the economic and political interests which supported drinking culture were growing in political influence parallel with the increasing distribution of their commercial product.

Thus, for seventy years, there had been in operation, with more or less success, a great variety of preventive laws at local and state levels, that were handicapped by surrounding "wet territory" and the restrictions of inter-state commerce. They were a continuous occasion of controversy, political, social, and economic, and at the same time, a means of educating the public.

The number of these civic laboratories—or local option dry spots—grew rapidly and became a landslide after 1900. Then, with economic and business as well as educational, religious, and moral forces backing the appeal, the evidence from it with a great wealth of local territory standing as unanswerable argument, the final steady drive of prohibition by states began with Georgia in 1907. State after state followed. One, Alabama, reversed its decision, then re-enacted prohibition after six years. Six states that, on the first vote made prohibition state-wide by small majorities, greatly increased those majorities at later plebiscites.

Drive for National Action

By 1917, when the 18th Amendment was submitted to Congress, twenty-five states had state-wide prohibition; eight others had the measure so far along that success was assured. Thousands of local communities, counties, towns, and cities in all the remaining states had banished saloons. There was not a state that did not have large areas free from liquor selling. More than fifty-six million, or 61% of the population, were living under prohibition laws of one type or another. Many great industries, such as iron and steel, had such heavy restrictions against drink as to be, in effect, a form of industrial banishment. Bankers, farmers, and several great labor organizations, were adding their support to the educational, religious and anti-liquor organizations that led the movement. Scientific information was becoming more available to the public. The popular magazines, newspapers, and latest books were filled with the subject—pro and con. It was thus that prohibition reached the national level.

To amend the Constitution, the most difficult possible way of doing so was followed. This required a two-thirds vote of each house of Congress, followed by ratification by three-fourths of all the states. The basic methods of American democracy were followed in full detail. Hasty action was nearly impossible.

The final decision was overwhelming. Not thirty-six, but forty-five states ratified the amendment; the three failing to do so contained only 5% of the population of the United States.

The Congressmen and Senators who voted to submit the amendment had been elected with prohibition as a national issue. All votes were *the votes of men.* Except in Colorado and one other state, women did not have the privilege of voting.

To repeat a statement at the beginning of this chapter in slightly different words: National Prohibition did not come suddenly to America. On the contrary, whatever else is said about it, its coming was not unexpected. The change was gradual, covering a period of more than a hundred years. It was an evolution, not a revolution. It reflected the growth of a large non-drinking section of society, a heavy majority at that time.

The total situation was well stated by Edward A. Ross, sociologist, University of Wisconsin:[4]

> What happened among us was that a part of American society turned away from liquor while the rest became wetter and wetter. The army of drinkers which survived the temperance typhoon of the "forties and fifties" of the last century had been re-enforced by millions of immigrants—Irish, German, and Slavs—many of whom, owing to their relatively high earnings in this country, found themselves able for the first time to indulge freely in alcoholic pleasures.
>
> Another momentous thing happened—a profound change in the system for supplying drink. The catering of liquor became commercialized. It came to be a big business, intent on profits—always more profits. From being shrinking and apologetic, it became brazen and aggressive. It no longer pleaded humble for leave to assuage existing thirsts. In order to "promote business," it deliberately and methodically set itself to create new thirsts. It advertised, gave away samples, subsidized convinial organizations, encouraged festal customs of a "damp" character, planted saloons in new places, and brought them into close partnership with the great social plagues, gambling and prostitution. . . . But as production and distribution were centralized, the business grew more capitalistic and the saloon keeper came to be the brewer's man, systematic efforts were made to "shove" liquor, especially beer. . . .
>
> Far then, from being a gratuitous stroke at a dying social custom, prohibition was an *urgent social defense measure forced by greedy liquor interests* which were so shortsighted that they would not leave the non-drinkers alone. Continually, they plotted to tempt the public into a larger consumption. Their ambition seemed to be to convert the rising generation of males into peripatetic tanks.
>
> A long and variegated experience with attempts to regulate the liquor traffic showed that it was incapable of being made decent and law-abiding. It would respect no law, heed no warnings or protests.

The prohibition of beverage alcohol came to America as the natural result of slowly growing public opinion with a hundred years of experimentation. It was a response to intelligent public demand. It gained its place only after overcoming relentless opposition. It made its case before the American public. Progress was orderly, steady, and, on the whole, very slow; yet, it culminated quickly after 1912.

It was democratic action of a people, who, at that period, refused to have the future of the nation, its economic, moral, and social welfare alike handicapped at almost every front of progress by drunkenness and a great economic interest that profitted from drunkenness.

4. "As the Sociologist Sees It", *The International Student,* October, 1921.

CHAPTER XI

RESTUDYING, REVISING AND REWRITING IN THE THIRTIES AND FORTIES

Seek the Truth
Come whence it may
Lead where it will.

IN THE FIRST EXCITING YEARS of our national prohibition experiment after 1919, hasty thinking people believed that the problem of alcoholic drink had been solved, settled constitutionally as it was, and that the country was on the way to social welfare settlement with the aid of the Eighteenth Amendment. After 1931 and again after 1934, the majority were equally sure that it was "all over" because of the Twenty-first Amendment.

The time certainly had come for re-study and an emphasis that would seek to discover more deeply, more objectively, yet realistically, what it was all about; what were the sources and forces of the cult of intoxication and, on the other hand, the understanding of these basic sources that had so steadily preceded this reform for a century in the United States. A great sociological experiment had been made. What could be learned from it?

A new approach had become imperative. Drinking customs were sweeping back. Older drinkers and the younger people who had known only the bootleggers and did not accept his trade were taking freely to legalized liquor.

Quotations from an advertisement in the *Brewery Industry,* November 19, 1932, just as repeal became effective, point out: "Half the expected market for beer does not exist today. When beer comes back, what is the first step brewers will take to restore temperate drinking among the youth of the land . . . Obviously there must be a campaign of education, and the one field in which this can be conducted is fortunately, the most important for immediate and future business, the colleges. Not one-tenth of the youth in college know what really good American beer tastes like."

After 1933, change came rapidly. By 1937, a survey by *The Literary Digest* revealed "a great boom in student drinking". A period of unrestrained distribution and changing customs in a large part—but only a part—of the public brought young people into contact with more free-flowing quantities of alcoholic drink than there ever had been before in North America.

From this situation came a new challenge to the Intercollegiate Association in 1933 to 1942, after national control had been transferred to the state governments which, in turn, often began to evade responsibility.

Seeking Leadership by Higher Education

Out of our earlier experience, we asked: What group is better, or as well qualified to lead in a new approach as are the colleges, the faculty members, the students, the alumni, the men and women who stand for leadership in public education on all such problems and seek to make it vital in the affairs of the nation? No other can so naturally take the longer view, the real one, in this struggle for release from the cult of intoxication!

Why should not the colleges at this critical time, raise standards that are scientific and in harmony with modern education of procedures on this problem, in the community, the state, and the college field itself? Encourage students to seek an intelligent basis for personal and group decision, based on growing scientific knowledge, instead of social group suggestion and pressure? Should not the great body of alumni, who have not forgotten the inspiring motives of their own college days, lead in educational service in their professional and business positions on this as they do in other great civic and national questions of the day.

Certainly, the time was ripe for a forward program based on the increasing scientific knowledge that had now become available as never before.

Preparing for a New Approach

By 1934, the Association had begun preparation for deeper study and a wider understanding of the problems of alcohol. Through the next ten years, we prepared new educational material that would include, more fully, the latest results of scientific research and its sociological applications. While seeking to be objective in our preceding years, we had, and I think wisely, centered attention realistically on those aspects of the problems that had been most closely related to the service needs of each particular period. The new program, therefore, would require a broader overall plan for studying the total problem as it appeared at that period.

The first reactions that came to many of us as we began to seek a more comprehensive program of education, after the sale of beverage alcohol had been re-legalized in 1933, were that in a very few years the public would see again the serious social disorders of the saloon era and that the favorable results of the thirteen testing years would so stand out that there would be a reaction against the reaction. Most of the average citizens who had supported the amendment from the first did not believe it had been a failure. Many people were confident that it had been as successful as could be expected from the trial of so great a sociological reform. But when repeal came, with so great a majority vote and so quickly, it became clear that there had been a real reversal of public opinion—that the people had "changed their minds".

For whatever may be the decision of future scientific historians who view more objectively the changes of the "Noble Experiment", as President Hoover called it in 1928, there were constructive results that have meaning for the future. The sale of legal alcohol just before prohibition in 1916-19, measured in absoluate alcohol content was 1.98 gallons per capita; it had been reduced to .47 gallons per capita by 1934.[1] Millions of families were using the drink money for other purposes; old alcoholics were dying off; sales promotion had been severely reduced; immature, ignorant personalities, children, and the overly frustrated were under less pressure from newspaper, magazine, and radio advertising. There was serious violation of all anti-liquor laws, but this worked both ways—to stimulate enforcement and better education on the one hand, and go against continuation of the prohibition policy on the other.

Through the fortunate foresight of Dr. Ernest H. Cherrington, President of the Association, we had begun as early as 1928 to prepare for a program that would be more lasting than were some parts of the IPA propaganda of earlier years. Through the World League Against Alcoholism, Dr. Cherrington offered to give a $100 set of books, pamphlets and reports free to 1,000 college and university libraries. The books related to all aspects of the problem, scientific, social, economic, historical, and international; there were 180 volumes, pamphlets, and smaller publications.

Outstanding in the set was the new *Standard Encyclopedia of The Alcohol Problem,* published a year earlier, after twenty years of American

1. Selected Statistic Tables, Rutgers Center, 1963.

and European research. The six large volumes covered particularly the history of the efforts in North America, Europe, and throughout the world to understand and deal with the problem. The Association supervised the distribution, selected the colleges, and arranged shipment. Within three years, 950 libraries had been supplied, a permanent investment for study of the world problems of alcoholic drink and two hundred years of attempts to deal with them.

First Consulting Group

On December 7, 1935, a representative group of twenty-five leading students, faculty members, and college organization officers from the colleges in and around Philadelphia met at Haverford college in an all-day discussion of the situation in colleges in the first two years after the sale of liquor had been nationally re-legalized.

The conference included a college president, a nationally known athletic coach, a dean of men, an expert forum-discussion leader among colleges, a medical expert, a chaplain, and secretaries from Christian Associations, the president of a senior class, a leader of college women, twelve students from various classes, and a secretary of the Intercollegiate Association.

Speaking from his position as a college President, Dr. W. W. Comfort, Haverford, discussed the recent growth of drink customs in influential social circles, and emphasized the strength of these customs in extending the drink habit among young people, especially among young women. He also gave instances of what it means when social leaders withstand this new fad and plan parties, teas, and other events without feeling it necessary to depend on alcohol to stir up sociability.

A message from Lawson Robertson, Olympic Track Coach at the University of Pennsylvania, who was unable to be present because of an injury, said that the athletic trainers in colleges and high schools of the United States, and practically all other countries are opposed to the use of alcohol by athletes at any time during training and many throughout the year; that in Germany 500,000 young men were training for the Olympic games, all of them on the "water-wagon" even as to beer.

Dr. John R. Hart, reporting college attitudes found on a tour he had just completed among the colleges of Ohio, Illinois, and California, said that students, teachers, and citizens he had met were concerned about the increasing drinking, especially by young women. In Iowa and other central states, a reaction had begun against this as "the smart thing to do".

Father Albers, Dean of Men at Villanova College, emphasized the *lasting value* of the *personal influence* of leaders and teachers toward restraining drink evils.

Emphasizing the importance of a new scientific approach to the problem, as a representative of the Intercollegiate Association, I said it would make possible study and discussion of all vital phases and lead to preparation for intelligent service in the community in after-college days. I called on professors and alumni to lead in this new approach.

Russell Callow, coach at the University of Pennsylvania, referred to the satisfaction he had in training students who do not drink and ended with the observation that it always makes the poor poorer. Dana A. How, University of Pennsylvania Christian Association, and A. K. Van Tine, Drexel Institute, brought out important attitudes and questions from experience in large bodies of students.

Frederick S. Bigelow, editorial writer for a great weekly magazine, discussed from forty years' study and experience the habit as it relates to young men and their future, calling beer "The Prize Time-Waster". He acknowledged that there are many pleasant things connected with drinking but thought it also tends to become a handicap to the best service in life.

In the discussion sessions, it was made clear that the educational method, including all important phases, is the only suitable approach among students, that one-sided emphasis would be received as an attempt to convert rather than to educate.

The fact and recent growth of the use of drink as a means of sociability and personal releases were discussed from various angles.

The effects of alcoholic drink in moderate and large quantities were presented by a practicing physician. Social responsibility for the consequences of drinking by auto-drivers and men who control machinery was recognized. Responsibility for the social consequences among the underprivileged and the undereducated and society in general aroused differences of opinion. Some said that drink would "make the poor man poorer" and the influence of the educated classes should be against it. Others refused to follow this reasoning and favored complete freedom for the self-controlled without regard to others.

There was a general impression that no solution, legal or educational, had yet been found; that law had failed and that education had not gone far enough to be effective. Some thought that alcoholism and heavy drinking were found chiefly among the underprivileged, and that in the upper classes there were not many who go to excess.

The major problem as it appeared in this conference was that frequent and heavy drinking was very serious; that moderate use was comparatively inoffensive, but as an aim, ineffective.

Carrying the question of social responsibility further, there seemed to be agreement that as long as there are people morally interested who keep everlastingly at it, a solution will be found; but if there is no moral side, then some other solution must be found, since the question will not solve itself.

New Studies

The first studies prepared to begin a "new approach" was a series of ten "Liquor and Social Welfare", revised to include the latest results of scientific research, published in *The International Student* in 1933 to 1936. Suggesting advance that had already begun, these studies included such themes as: "Rethinking the Problem Today", "Alcohol Release in Life Today", "What Social Consequences Has Alcoholic Beverage?", "Should Drink Customs Be Encouraged?".

"Alcohol Trends in College Life" was a survey of attitudes and practices in the preceding three-quarters of a century. This 48-page pamphlet had a circulation of 77,000 among instructors, college pastors, and Christian student associations. "The College and Drink Today" expressed the need for educational leadership; "Alcoholic Drink in Life Today", a five-study outline for group discussions, had a circulation of 70,000. Articles with similar content were being published by church publications.

The most adventurous of these was a series of 16 "New Understanding Monographs", or popular-style studies on particular social aspects; "Is Alcohol the Same Old Problem?", "Slump and Resurgence in Liquor Culture", "Alcoholic Expression and Personality", "Alcoholic Culture: Should It Be Retained?", "World Questioning of Alcoholic Pleasure", "Alcoholic Release and Public Disorder", "Alcoholic Release and Public Safety".

It had become clear, under the slogan, "Seek the Truth, Come Whence It May", that had caught the attention of my associates and myself, that our search would be long, far beyond the lifetime of any of us, young and old, who had been making the first known attempt in that direction. For six years, I continued studying at the Library of Congress, in search of the deeper sources, the history and the culture of alcohol in human society. With me were associated at that period two very keen young men with whom I had frequent discussions: John H. Shouse, Berea College, 1931, a student of Law at George Washington University, Secretary of the Association, and Edwin H. Maynard, Cornell College, 1938, associate in writing, who later became editor of one of the largest religious publications in the United States. These recent students kept me in close touch with the changing attitudes in the colleges during this re-writing period. Their younger thinking had much to do with the growth of our new understanding of the problem as we shared those years together working it out.

Cultural Sources

Consequently, the attention of the Association was being turned more and more to the traditions and the psychological motivations that had been overlooked or minimized during the years that legislation had been the main idea in the reform.

These were expressed at the time in an editorial in *The International Student:*

> The seeking of pleasure in the "kick" of alcohol has a large—almost dominant—place in (certain sections of) society and daily living. The sensations to be gained, mild or vivid, are popular sources of enjoyment, ease and escape from discomfort and the facts of reality, today as in the childhood of the race. But ever and always alcoholic pleasure has been questioned, among all people, in all ages. Only recently has this world-wide challenge of critical-minded and socially-interested men been supplemented by a scientific challenge to the basic value of alcoholic pleasure—of what it is, what it does, and how it does it.

Thus, it became clear to us in the Association that any program in our field must now be more realistic—include the motives of those who used it—more understanding than in the past. "Temperance", "abstinence", "moderation", "freedom to drink", "control", "local option", "prohibition", were all limited concepts—that, together with our great national experience, all pointed to the need for more study and for frank recognition of the deeper and most persistent sources. This encompassed the tradition of drink culture and its relation as a source to the demands of modern public safety, health, and social welfare.

To challenge and by frank analysis to begin to study the culture of alcohol in the community and the nation, and to popularize non-alcoholic customs and satisfactions now became a vision of the future.

There comes to me personally after 64 years, a vision of the future—a long-time vision—for how can the states of intoxication, mild, excessive, or compulsive, have a natural place in normal human living? The specific desire for alcohol has to be created anew in each generation. Social customs and trade propaganda continue to initiate and enlarge anesthetic desires, create habits of dependence and elevate a substitutional, often degrading, satisfaction into something romantic and important. Alcoholic satisfaction and release from unhappy feelings, large or small, conceal but do not remove any source of these ills. Resort to it may be discarded because of the never-ending supply of new addicts, accidents, ill health, mental instability, crime, and degraded personality that comes from it.

But—"Face the Responsibility"

Nevertheless, the major sector of our culture today continues to accept, a substantial minority continues to reject, this basic factor in all alcoholic drink problems in the western cultures of today.

Recognizing the challenge in the slogan, "Seek the Truth, Lead Where It Will", the Association came to include and emphasize a frank discussion policy as the only method of encouraging study. It placed its faith in the decisions that young men and women must make reasonable study. This approach, not only insures personal and group decision where it belongs, it also adds the responsibility of doing so, and doing it intelligently with a sense of concern that goes far beyond individual self-seeking. It is the decision of mature and socially conscious citizens—to the end that the acquiring of a dependable working knowledge obviously becames the first requirement—*the modern approach.*

This policy was published in the *International Student,* May, 1939, under the title, "A Neglected Emphasis", as follows:

> There is one emphasis—a new one—that may be made in the present situation in the United States, that has in it *un-measured possibilities of creative leadership.* It is to face the "facts" as they are, study the basic realities of the whole problem of alcoholic drink in society and do it comprehensively. . . . This is an approach to this highly controverted issue that has not been given much attention in the century or more of earnest effort to find a solution. . . .
>
> Much is being done and proposed to relieve the unfortunate consequences of alcohol, but little that seeks the sources from which they come. It is not sufficient to promote public safety, to stop drinkers from driving and tipsy walkers from walking, to restrain heavy drinking, or to cure "problem drinkers". All of this—and much more—is good curative service.
>
> Why not go further—to the sources—ask and discuss freely such questions as:

What are the satisfactions that men seek when they drink? What do they get when they obtain them? Why create the desire for narcotic and esthetic pleasure in the first place? Should social drink customs be freely accepted or questioned? Where do they come from? How are they made popular? How strong is the force of profit-seeking back of the popular promotion? What about narcotic pleasure as a source of gain, private or public? What are the costs? Why should influential society lead the community and the nation into practices that are certain to result in disaster to millions—those very millions who suffer most, who feel most the needs which alcohol satisfies?

And why should not the prestige of social drinking be questioned—the drinking at alumni banquets, formal dinners, cocktail parties, the clubs of "big business", and lesser business, the afternoon gatherings of the socially elite? Why should not these customs be evaluated in the light of practical experience . . . of how they dominate the lives of millions who follow unthinking the fashions of the "privileged"? Why not analyze realistically—or debunk—the welter of literary and social traditions that have grown close around the pleasure of alcoholic intoxication through the ages?

Such a program of education is based on modern methods, instead of those of the reformer. It will create occasions for united thinking and action, examine questionable customs and help to create intelligent public opinion. It will face modern liquor problems at their *most popular and least understood sources. . . .*

First New Approach Conference: Washington, 1941

It was to study frankly the post-repeal situation in college communities that our first conference of educators and students convened in Washington, in 1941, two years before the first Yale School of Alcohol Studies was announced. Those who attended were seeking a new statement of purpose for the Association as a base for future education at the college level.

As a conference, not of reformers or the politically inclined, it tried to be objective and scientific. It included professors and students; a national leader in college religious education, a state school board educator, the officers of the Association, young and old. It gave particular attention to the bearing that scientific, especially psychological, investigation, and modern educational theories should have in efforts to reduce alcoholic intoxication and its consequences. Small in numbers, but unified in purpose, it faced the most critical phases of the problem of the post-repeal days.

As a first attempt to find and launch a constructive program in harmony with the recent educational ideas, the conference gave attention to the responsibility that college leadership might now take in the future, since public thinking had been removed from the legal to the educational and scientific aspects of the problem.

"What is the Beverage Alcohol Problem of Today?" was the question asked by Dr. Gould Wickey, Executive Secretary of the National Church Boards of Education. Following in natural sequences were: "The Influence of Recent Scientific and Psychological Understanding", "Alcohol Culture", "How to Get Thinking People to Think for Themselves". Neither political nor legal issues had any part in this meeting.

The significance of taking into account the motives that prompt men to drink, especially youth and younger people; the importance of satisfying those needs in natural ways; and the influence of social customs and the desire for ease and freedom in self-expression as forces that start and continue habits of toxic pleasure that lead to drinking were brought out by Dr. Albion Roy King.

Discussing the place of the college, Professor Raymond E. Mendenhall, Education, Otterbein College, said that instruction alone does not offer a solution, that "attitudes are caught rather than taught. Nothing is sinful if everyone is doing it. Here we have the root of our present orgy of social drinking . . . style . . . the persistent efforts of the mass to conform to the customs of the few persons of prestige."

Representing the younger conferees, John H. Shouse, George Washington Law, 1937, Secretary of the Association, said, "People refuse to think. If students and young people are once made conscious of the problems, if we get them to thinking, we need not worry about what their conclusions will be." This conviction was echoed by Edwin H. Maynard, Cornell College, who stated that he found intelligent and sincere discussion among students, when they gave attention to it, but that the vast majority fail to see any need for discussion at all.

"Most people believe that the problem of liquor was settled by repeal of the Eighteenth Amendment. Students and professors do not see as much drinking as other groups and therefore are not made as conscious, of it," said Lloyd M. Bertholf, Dean of Men at Western Maryland College. I cited prestige that has been acquired by drink customs in recent years through the influence of social leaders and the effect of propaganda. Howard E. Hamlin, Professor of Health and Narcotics, Ohio State Department of Education, agreed, citing examples of prominent educators and church men. From his experience in schools, he reported that children in the elementary grades and youth in high schools are interested in receiving factual, scientific teaching on alcohol.

That interest lags among men of college age was an opinion of President Carl D. Smith, Babson Institute. "The lack of appreciation of the relation between the use of alcohol and the problems of life that they will have to face after leaving the campus. They do not realize the extent to which it may affect their possibility of getting a job." He suggested that in these practical applications of the problem, "we have fallen down." Professor Mendenhall, agreeing, emphasized the force of social influence, the "everybody's doing it", and other drives of a social pressure nature.

Dr. King pictured the average student as having a determination to drink and to be temperate. "Never has drunkenness been more in bad repute," he declared, "or rebellion against abstinence so nearly 100%."

Dr. Ernest H. Cherrington, President of the Association, noted an absence on both sides of "a generally accepted definition of what the alcohol problem is. Our opinions are indefinite. Each one is afraid to speak until he has heard the other fellow's viewpoint." But he added a new and positive challenge for the future when he said that the present situation represents a more healthful viewpoint than did the direct clash of earlier periods when dogmatism prevailed.

Summing up, Dr. Wickey pointed out where the program of the Intercollegiate Association could be especially helpful. "The lack of awareness," he said, "of the problem and the passivity in the home and in the church, all point to the need of such an educational program . . . to awaken a new interest among those who should be concerned."

"The time has come to seek the cooperation of both faculty members and students, in educational service and leadership on the alcohol problem *to an extent never before* undertaken," wrote Dr. Charles A. Ellwood, sociologist of Duke University, to the 1941 conference following his study of the situation in the first eight years after the sale of alcoholic beverages had been re-legalized.

"It is of vital importance," wrote Dr. S. Ralph Harlow, Smith College, "that more thought and education be given this growing problem and its relation to our educational system."

"But the attitude of college teachers," wrote President George B. Cutten, Colgate, "is most discouraging. Otherwise people of fine influence, their attitude on that account is all the more disastrous." An educator who was giving full time to the scientific understanding of the problem in teachers' colleges and high schools wrote, "I am becoming more and more discouraged with the presentation of the alcohol problem to older students. They tell me again and again, 'We have enough facts.' But they seem to *lack a desire to act upon the facts they have.* They want facts that have 'meaning.'"

Social Prestige Patterns

To examine frankly the influence of the social patterns set by those who extol as a privilege, without concern as to consequences, the traditional drink customs of polite society, should now be a job for research.

These customs and sanctions spread out from prestige groups by imitation to all those who seek to climb to similar positions of influence and higher income. Broadcasting nightly to the millions and millions over television and radio, movies, and glamorous trade advertising, the drink culture becomes a vast sifting process that initiates, then holds many who count on it, personally and for party entertainment, until without knowledge of what is happening, a sense of dependence, even addiction, has been fully established.

For some at all levels of daily living, this habit of looking to alcohol for what it gives is not or cannot be broken until a stage is reached that requires the aid of a specialist. In every group, of course, there are many who are not appreciably affected, but the number that are is serious. As a sifting out process of those who are susceptible to alcoholic excess, the customs of a community constitute a fundamental source of the problem.

The distributors, the "carriers" of the illness to those of little or no resistance, are the drink customs with group approvals back of them. They spread among those who are susceptible, the peculiar desire, which for many individuals in every generation, may slowly or quickly become dominant over the desire for food, clothing, family, and self-respect—as vividly seen in "The Lost Weekend".

The Overlooked or Unthinking Sources

In a lecture at the first Yale School, Dr. E. N. Jellinek reported later that "Among excessive drinkers, from 10 to 20 per cent have become excessive only after the development of a mental disorder. To these, inebriety is only a sympton. More important is the individual who has no mental disorder, but who deviates from the normal sufficiently to solve his conflicts in socially unacceptable ways. But this so-called problem drinker also forms only a small part of the inebriate population. The largest part appears to come from entirely normal origins, brought to excess through social factors, rather than personality factors. Ultimately they, too, become medical problems. Primarily, therefore, inebriety is a social problem which, secondarily, takes on medical aspects."

From these backgrounds of later research constantly renewed, the Association has been working, in recent years. The purposes of the "new approach" that had been maturing within the Intercollegiate Association thus came to have a more scientific foundation from the beginning. "Seek the truth fearlessly, wherever it may be found; Study—then decide. Promote study and discussion, in college, the community, city, state and nation."

Chapter XII

A NEW UNDERSTANDING BEGINS TO FUNCTION

THE WASHINGTON CONFERENCE of June 20, 1941, was a natural outgrowth of the psychological and cultural knowledge relating to alcohol in human living that had been maturing slowly among us of the Association after 1932, and the adoption of the scientific spirit—"Seek the Truth, Lead Where It Will". In the light of this new understanding, the leaders of the Association had been quietly restudying the problem of alcohol in society for several years, seeking an approach that could be educationally effective under the changes that were occurring in public attitude and opinion.

The objectives that stood out after this conference included: (1) Renew study and instruction on the whole problem; (2) Seek closer cooperation with teachers of sociology, psychology, history, health, and philosophy; (3) Promote scientific and objective study of the problem in all of its aspects; (4) Compile and distribute information on what is being done in colleges; (5) Encourage forum discussion and analysis of the present situation; and (6) Encourage young men and women to seek positions of service related to the alcohol problem.

The appeal was to thinking people, to all who were not afraid to face the situation and the implication of the facts: personal, social, and practical; to all who would base opinion and service on a new and more scientific understanding of the meaning of intoxication and drink and had the faith to put the convictions into their living.

Initiate and cooperate with college faculty members and student leaders in setting up local campus seminars or clinics and in areas, conferences of leaders, with outstanding speakers of scientific and educational ability, counselors, and student leaders as participants. Emphasize an open-minded approach and unlimited discussion in this educational project.

Yale School Offers a Meaningful Understanding

Then came the Yale School of Alcohol Studies, July, 1943. Dr. Albion

R. King, Professor Howard E. Hamlin, and I attended the five weeks of scientific and historical lectures, shared freely in all discussions, seminars, and the spontaneous bull sessions in the evenings under the trees of the Divinity School Campus.

Out of those weeks came a renewed sense of confidence in the program we had been planning and so far had been leading. There came, also, many new understandings of the personal and public health consequences, particularly psychological, of alcohol in human living. Here, it came to us, was an approach that would "mean something" to the most indifferent, the most sophisticated in the general public and in the college communities. The health and safety emphasis would make it realistic to students, the mental illness of "the alcoholic", the heavy drinker, and the indifference of the drinking culture to the people of that culture.

Organized to bring out for education service the results of modern scientific research and study, and to correct popular misconceptions relating to beverage alcohol and its influence in personal and human living, the new Summer Course in Alcohol Studies at Yale University was the first instance of highly objective and critical study of the problem of alcohol ever offered to the public by a great university in this country or in any other. The health and safety emphasis made it realistic.

This gave to Yale a place of constructive leadership in the objective approach to the problem already begun by critical leaders in the United States and Canada and marked it as the outstanding event relating to the problem of alcohol in the middle half of the twentieth century.

The course of study at Yale was always of graduate rank. It was the conviction of the founders that there was unused scientific information filed away in university libraries. This knowledge had too long been kept for academic use alone; it should now be brought out, together with additions from current research, given to the public, and made available for educational purposes.

The first course in June and July, 1943, was announced as one for high school and college educators, professional, public health, and medical men, temperance workers, writers, managers of liquor control boards, representatives of the industry, doctors, nurses, and others seriously interested. For five weeks, representatives from all these ways of thinking lived in the dormitories, listened to the lectures, questioned the speakers, shared vigorously in the seminars and the spontaneous discussion groups every evening under the trees on the lawn and in the rooms of the students. Whenever Dr. E. N. Jellinek appeared, a questioning group attached itself to him. He was not only a research specialist, but such a magnetic person that whenever he appeared on the walks or grass of the quadrangle he was quickly surrounded by a deeply inquiring—and sometimes argumentative—group. Beyond all the lectures, I will never forget those open air discussions.

The faculty of the school were all recognized specialists in their particular fields. They were from the United States Department of Public Health, the faculties of Yale, Harvard, Columbia and leaders in education and legislation and from hospitals who had been giving practical service in previous years.

At the orientation, Dr. Jellinek made a very clarifying statement when he said that "science cannot solve the alcohol problem, only people can do that, but science can help." Dr. Howard H. Haggard, director, made it clear that the approach of the school would be strictly scientific; that a scientific attitude would be encouraged at all points and that the whole project of Yale was to provide scientific knowledge for the use of the public, but not to engage in any program of education as such.

The New Health Emphasis

To recognize alcoholism, as a question of health, and the confirmed alcoholic and excessive drinkers as emotionally, mentally, and sometimes physically ill, had already given the problem a decisive place in public health. It was no longer just a question of intemperance or the voting out of saloons. As a subject of health, it demanded and had begun to receive a more and more positive, dignified status in public attention, for alcoholism had already become, in the view of high public leaders, one of the four greatest health problems of America.

That alcoholism is a plague to health is a scientific concept of recent years. It is now recognized as one of the four greatest public health disorders of recent years. The antics of an intoxicated person at a party, saloon, or home can never be taken lightly as a mere immorality or misdemeanor that ends with a night in jail. Too often the conduct of a drunken person is the expression of an inner condition that marks him as mentally and emotionally, if not physically, ill.

Several years before Yale, Dr. Winfred Overholser, St. Elizabeth's Hospital, Washington, D.C., described the situation in these words: "With tuberculosis, cancer, syphilis, mental disease, and polio receiving competent and intelligent medical attention, we now have alcoholism as the greatest public health problem of the present time that is not being systematically attacked."

It is now better known that many men and women who are alcoholics or on the way to becoming alcoholics through heavy drinking have personal traits, emotional instabilities, or deep feelings of inadequacy. They seem unable to face the demands of daily living. They are more susceptible to alcohol than the average person. But many others—the majority of all inebriates and addicts—have become what they are as a result of their years of habitual or social drinking. By one or a combination of routes come the alcohol-sick.

It has been estimated that 40 to 50% of the alcoholics in the United States are such because of personality deficiencies; that about 60% have reached this stage through years of moderate or excessive drinking. Probably, a similar ratio prevails among the 4,000,000 inebriates.

As "sick people", confirmed alcoholics may be compared with the half-million each of tubercular and cancerous patients in this country, which in number, they greatly exceed. "The rich and the poor, the highly intellectual and ignorant, the frail and the robust, the shy and the apparently bold, the worried and the seemingly carefree, all furnish their quota of inebriates," wrote a leading psychiatrist.

Most vital is the effect of alcohol in the functioning of the central nervous system. Even before drinking becomes "excessive" in the ordinary use of the word, mental activities are depressed to a degree that cannot be called healthful. In advanced cases, it is to the hospitals for mental disorders and the sanitariums that shield wealthy inebriates that we look for the results of alcoholic culture, as well as the stream of repeating drunks from the police courts.

From the five weeks of intensive study, there came a better understanding of man's long dependence on alcohol as a drug of escape—a history of why they have counted on it so heavily. Ever since our primitive ancestors, in search of food, discovered that decaying fruits and grains provide an exciting "kick" to their feelings, a substantial part of each generation has been seeking alcoholic pleasure. From it they have gained both happiness and misery.

Overlooked or Unthinking Sources

At the School, that first year, Dr. E. N. Jellinek stated in a lecture that "among excessive drinkers, from 10 to 20% have become excessive only after the development of a mental disorder. To these, inebriety is only a symptom. More important is the individual who has no mental disorder, but who deviates from the normal sufficiently to solve his conflicts in socially unacceptable ways. But this co-called problem drinker also forms only a small part of the inebriate population. The largest part appears to come from entirely normal origins, brought to excess through social factors, rather than personality factors. Ultimately they, too, become medical problems. Primarily, therefore, inebriety is a social problem which, secondarily, takes on medical aspects."

It is from these backgrounds of research, constantly renewed later, that the Intercollegiate Association has been working in recent years. The "new approach" that has been maturing within the philosophy and program of the Association has come to have a more fundamental foundation as a result of the slogan: "Seek the truth fearlessly, wherever it may be found." Study—then decide. Promote study and discussion, in college, the community, city, state and nation.

Beginnings to "Popularize"

It was with this in mind that the Intercollegiate Association immediately thereafter began to put into educational circulation much of the basic material that came from the Yale School. In our own periodical first, *The International Student,* circulating in colleges, libraries, among faculty members and student leaders, and 10,000 or more public high schools; *The Scientific Temperance Journal,* of which I was acting editor for ten years; and *The Voice,* temperance journal of the Methodist Church of which I was a writer, a continuous series of articles and condensations of lectures given at the first Yale School. These conference lectures, along with several additional lectures, were published in 1944 by the *Quarterly Journal of Alcohol Studies,* as *The Abridged Lectures of the First Summer Course (1943) of Alcohol Studies at Yale University.*

In the 1944 School, I shared in a panel of three, Rev. Francis W. McPeek, Council of Churches, New York, and Dr. E. N. Jellinek, on "The Philosophy of the Temperance Movement". That year, the lectures at the summer school were recorded and published in full in *Alcohol, Science, and Society,* the first complete report of a session of the school.

Spreading the Pattern

In 1945, January 29, several of us from Columbus who had attended the first Yale School, Howard E. Hamlin, Director of Alcohol Education in the high schools of the state (representing the Ohio Department of Education), and I, in cooperation with Dr. C. C. North, Sociology, Ohio State University, organized a one-day program at Ohio State University. Dr. E. N. Jellinek and Dr. Selden D. Bacon were invited to come and lead a Yale style, one day pilot program. It was one of the first extension programs of this type in the Mid-west. Many others followed in college centers.

In his introductory statement, Dr. C. C. North stated:

> As you are all quite aware, the question of alcohol has been so highly controversial in the United States that we have become accustomed to think of it in terms of controversy. The men from the Yale School of Alcohol Studies are therefore pioneers in approaching a controversial subject apart from controversy and in subjecting it to as objective and scientific analysis as is given to other social problems . . . and that is the whole point of view of the conference—that we want to understand the problem and to see it in its relation to other aspects of American Life.

This central Ohio conference was sponsored by the Ohio State Department of Education and by the University Departments of Sociology, Social Administration, Education at Ohio State, and the University Religious Council. Dr. Frank Stradley, Vice-President of the University was chairman. The organizing was done from the office of the Intercollegiate Association by Professor Howard E. Hamlin and myself. A report was published by the Division of Health and Narcotics of the State Board of Education with the title: *Popularizing the Educational Approach to the Problems of Alcohol* and sent to all the high schools and colleges of Ohio. The meaning is illustrated by the themes and names of the speakers: "The Role of the Public School", Fred C. Slager, Principal, Central High School, Columbus; "The Alcohol Problem: Its Complexity in Modern Life", E. N. Jellinek, D.Sc., Yale; "The Alcoholic: A Study in the Interplay of Individual and Social Factors", Selden D. Bacon, Ph.D., Yale; "Understanding the Alcoholic", George T. Harding, M.D., Harding Sanitarium, Worthington, Ohio; "Popularizing the Findings Concerning Alcohol", Dr. E. N. Jellinek; "The Function of the College", Dr. H. J. Burgstahler, President, Ohio Wesleyan University; "Alcoholics Anonymous", Rev. Floyd Faust, D.D.; and "Science and Alcohol", Dr. Jonathan Foreman, M.D., both of Columbus.

Faculty members and students in Central Ohio attended in representative numbers, despite an ice storm that made travel almost impossible. Two classes of 90 students from OSU came with their instructors.

The night before, Dr. Jellinek had finished a heavy day of conferences at Indianapolis, with a late night session. Trains were delayed by the storms; he could not obtain a sleeper to Columbus. Knowing that the train would arrive at about four a.m., I arranged to meet him when he reached a hotel. I joined him in the lobby, had numerous coffees, and called Mr. Hamlin, who came and took him to his home for a few hours rest before his first lecture. It was while we were waiting at the hotel that Dr. Jellinek suggested what some of us had been dreaming about—that the Association organize and conduct a "Little Yale School of Alcohol Studies" for college students. This we did in 1949-50, the first at Otterbein College, with a student, Stanley F. Knock, Jr., as Chairman.

In a Central Ohio College Conference, four years later, indication appeared that the new conception of Alcoholism as an "illness" and the Alcoholic, as "sick" was catching attention in college communities as well as in the scientific centers. Also, drinking was a growing concern with deans of students. Our program included the purpose: "to strengthen educational and moral forces toward the prevention of Alcoholism."

Telling of his own experiences as a graduate student at OSU, a World War II veteran said:

> My drinking started here in Columbus when I was fourteen, a high school Sophomore. From there on until a year ago, I was continually drunk . . . an alcoholic . . . in order to get along, fit into any social group and yet keep on drinking. I took every opportunity . . . my one purpose in life was to drink. I have been sober a year now, yet I am only one drink away from where I was when drunk. . . . I am spending a great deal of time counseling with high school and college students. . . . I talked to 585 in 13 groups of juniors and seniors. Sixty-five percent asked questions that indicate a drinking problem in their immediate families—questions they do not ask their ministers, school advisers.

"College students who do not drink usually abstain on account of moral reasons, or scientific, or a combination of both; those who drink because they feel they have to, become chronic drinkers later in response to social invitation; they want to be seen in the 'right' place with the 'right' people . . . often the 'right place' is a bar."

This Forum Conference on "Education and the Problem Today, a Preventive Approach", was sponsored by the State Board of Education, the Colleges of Education, Medicine, and Welfare at Ohio State, the University Council of Religious Education, and Capital, Denison, Ohio Wesleyan Universities, Otterbein College, and the State Student Y.M. C.A., and the Intercollegiate Association.

"The Public Health Approach" was the theme of the lecture by Dr. Haven Emerson, Professor of Health, Columbia University, New York; "The Situation We Face Today" was discussed by Dr. Harold F. Titus,

Professor of Philosophy, Denison University; "The Cult of Alcohol in Social Tradition", Dr. Carl A. Nisson, Professor of Sociology, Ohio State; "The Situation as We See It", a panel discussion by an army veteran and a Y.M.C.A. secretary; "The Role of Public School Education on Alcohol", Dr. Fred C. Slager, Central High School, Columbus; "The Cult of Moderation in College Communities", Dean Albion Roy King, Cornell College, Mt. Vernon, Iowa; "College Students Face the Problem", Richard Richards, Ohio-West Virginia Y.M.C.A. College Secretary; "Church and Youth Leaders", Richard Bell, Director Christian Education, Community Church, Columbus, Ohio.

These two conferences, at Ohio State University in 1945 and at the City Y.M.C.A. in 1948, were significant to the Intercollegiate Association for several basic reasons. First, we were pioneering to find a base for a stable and enlarged program following the revival of heavy drinking in the period of interest in almost every phase of the alcohol problem after the repeal of the Eighteenth Amendment. Second, with scientific attention already centered on "the alcoholic" and the public health approach, we began to concentrate on these understandings in the college field. This we had begun to do twenty years earlier through our publications. Now, the time had come to demonstrate our original objectives.

The influence of these first conferences spread, both within and without our own field. This spread was wider than we could know at the time. A continuous stream of reports and articles in *The International Student* reached nearly all the colleges and, for ten years, was sent to 23,000 public high schools. In addition, Dr. King, Vice-President, was called on continuously for lectures on the meaning of the Yale School. I had calls for talks and edited study outlines for church and educational publications.

Editorial Writing Awards

Seeking to encourage study of the accumulating knowledge that had been coming from research centers regarding Alcohol in the previous twenty or more years, a Denver friend of the Association about 1945 offered awards of $500 for college students writing on "Applying Preventive Medicine to Alcoholism". The next year, he renewed the offer, using the subject, "Outgrowing Alcoholic Culture".

In 1947, Logan H. Roberts, a leading businessman of Yakima, Washington, gave first to the Pacific Northwest a long series of such awards, $500 for essays or editorials on "Campus Drinking Problems". Within three years, he set up an investment fund of $77,000 in a New York

Foundation, the proceeds to be used to continue these awards to undergraduates and to aid publication of the winning papers every year.

Roberts had come into the Association immediately after graduating in Law at New York University, in 1902, following his college years at Nebraska Wesleyan. Deeply devoted to the struggle against intemperance and the saloon, his early ideal had been to give life service to this cause. He gave three very active years traveling among colleges, then raised the first $500 the Association had yet received. Years later, he and his son, Donald, completed a permanent investment "to aid solution of the Alcohol Problem". These annual awards are a memorial to his life-service in law, business administration, and his church.

The winner of highest honors in 1964 was Miss Carol Beeman Bond of Louisiana State College, Monroe, La., who wrote on "Alcoholism and Mental Health".

Beginnings of the Intercollegiate Summer Schools

Out of the indications of growing interest among experienced leaders came the conviction, in 1949, that the time was ripe for launching a conference, or short summer school, particularly for undergraduate and recent graduate students. This would be strictly objective and give full freedom for the expression of opinion and discussion by students attending.

Organized by a self-appointed committee of the Association, each of whom seemed to have discovered the idea for himself, Dr. Albion R. King, Stanley F. Knock, a student at Yale School of Theology, Richard Richards, college Secretary for Ohio of the Y.M.C.A., and myself, it became the first "Little Yale School", a title suggested by Dr. E. N. Jellinek. The school was held August 27-September 1, 1950, at Otterbein College, Westerville, Ohio, by the Association. Stanley F. Knock, because he was a student, was made chairman and Edwin H. Maynard, Director of Group Seminars.

Material for study and discussion was given in daily lectures by experts as follow: "College Rules and Social Controls", "Psychological Effects of Alcohol", "Motivations", "What Medical Science has Learned About the Effect of Ethyl Alcohol on Man", "The Public Health Aspects of Alcoholism as a Preventable Disease", "Alcoholic Beverages: Social and Cultural Aspects", "The Role of Education in the Control of Alcohol", "Facing the Alcohol Problem on the College Campus", "New Plays for the Second Half", "As a Judge Sees 'The Drunk' and His Treatment",

"Spiritual Recovery of Alcoholic Persons", and "Abstinence Vs. Moderation as Ethical Principles".

Approval of this new project began to come at once after 1950. "The Intercollegiate School has had a profound effect on those who have been able to attend it . . . the need is for . . . more (so that) less official people can attend." "The most significant move that the Association has made in recent years." "I am wholly in accord with your method of approach and only hope that I can help in some significant way."

Following the first "Little Yale" at Otterbein in 1950, the second at Cornell College, Iowa, a session at the University of Toronto, one at the University of Chicago, Nebraska Wesleyan, and the University of Western Ontario, the International Intercollegiate School has been annually continued at McMaster University, Hamilton, Ontario, as the major project of the Association. It now includes in its program the latest findings of research and modern thinking such as the following at the School, August, 1964: "Why Be Concerned About Alcohol Problems?", "College Drinking Patterns", "Factors which Influence Motivations", "Alcohol and The Human Body", "Deviant Behavior and Alcohol", "The Nature of Addiction".

The McMaster International School of August 23-28, 1965 centered attention on two aspects of particular interest at the time, with successive lectures by Dr. George Maddox, Duke University, and Dr. Robert D. Russell, Stanford. Among the subjects discussed were: "Drinking Patterns in America"; "Free Wheeling"—a student reaction period following the preceding topic; "Physiological Aspects of Alcohol Use"; Psychological and Sociological Motives Regarding Alcohol"; "Implications of Drinking" and "What Part Do You Play?"

Chapter XIII

CONTINUING SOURCES OF ALCOHOLISM AND DISORDER

OUT OF THE STUDY GROUPS that the field secretaries of the association set up in the colleges they visited in the first two years after 1900, to equip students for some immediate project of service, the need for more basic study became increasingly evident. The students who had taken part in anti-alcohol campaigns, speaking or canvassing, had gained a desire for a fuller understanding of the problem than were the appeals that characterized much of the emotional denunciation and speaking of the opponents of the saloon and the liquor traffic. They wanted more objective study of the whole problem.

They wanted to know more about how it affected the body and mind. What alcohol and drinking meant to those who fully accepted it. The deeper desires for this particular drug. What was back of the saloon? And the effect of that drug in stimulating the sale of this article from which obviously came streams of intemperance, excess, and drunkenness. And they began to want scientific and objective knowledge from which to make life decisions not just public speeches. Objective factual study thus became the educational policy of the Association, even while thousands of our members were active in no-license, local option and other projects of applied service at different periods in later years.

Continuing Sources

Now today the practical question stands out: How does it happen that while the educational activities of a century and more have become objective and scientific, revolutionized, the general movement to reduce the tragedies of alcoholic excesses, alcoholism and its consequences, have not been more effective?[1] That the popularity of this particular drug has come to be as persistent, as wide-spread, as we see it today? Why are tragedies on the highway, beer-drinking by teen-agers, and the number of alcoholics increasing? Why has not our deeper understanding, our

1. William B. Terhune, M.D., "The Rising Tide of Alcoholism", *Reader's Digest,* June, 1965.

advanced research, the wider spread of our latest knowledge, the fellowship of A.A.'s, the service of psychiatrists, not been able to delay the trends in the annual production of the "alcoholic sick" Why is our present mass of tested knowledge not more freely accepted? A quick review of my observation of sixty-five years may renew the overall picture.

Drinking and alcoholism begin, continue and grow largely because of the Cult of Alcohol that prevails in modern society. This cult shows itself as background in the following ways:

1. The tradition of "Drink" that has come down from the past as something that seemingly is necessary in the lives of millions. The use of alcohol is embedded in the customs and mores of a large part of our total society.
2. Current social customs, prestige and fashions, that spread approvals, extend use and initiate and continue alcoholic satisfaction as something that is desirable.
3. The character of alcoholic satisfaction which is a drug-induced substitution that offers relief to emotional ills, frustrations, and physical disorders.
4. Economic pressures that seek to enlarge and intensify the alcoholic desire, once it has been created by tradition and usage.
5. A social sifting process has been created by the Alcohol Custom that selects and initiates into drinking those who are most susceptible to its dangers and many who, through frequent drinking, become susceptible.

Tradition of Toxic Joy

The tradition of alcoholic pleasure is deeply ingrained in the culture of America and most modern nations, as is, also, a powerful resistance culture.

Alcoholic beverages were both popular and unpopular, among the English, French, German, Swedish, Slavic, Italian and other peoples long before as immigrants they left their native lands—deep in the mores and daily practices of ages. Even the Puritans were drinkers in colonial days.

These drinking cults of the colonial and immigration periods were dominant in the Federal years until challenged by the beginnings of the first temperance and religious reaction against drunkenness and the tavern. Moderation and total abstinent movements appeared with thousands of local groups and hundreds of state societies through the nineteenth and first third of the twentieth centuries. With usual acceptance "drink" has remained since, a Cult in the Culture of today.

Among those who accept the tradition, behaviors are learned chiefly in childhood as are other patterns of conduct; the attitudes of the children are those of their parents and parental associates.

The classification and significance of the customs of the basic social groups in America as given by Dollard, sociologist, at the first Yale School of Alcohol Studies, are now generally accepted as an outline for study[2] of the cultural sources of drinking.

In the Upper-Upper long standing, old-family group, constituting but 2% of the population, drinking is usual, very extensive, by both sexes, a cultural but not a moral matter. It is done in party style, in the home and elsewhere. But there are stiff social controls against—not drunkenness—but anti-social or ungentlemanly conduct while intoxicated. The patterns of their conduct sift down to adults and groups in the lower strata.

Among the Lower-Upper, 2% of the population, drinking is more reckless and heavy. They are the families of new wealth; they feel frustrated in face of those above who "own society" and try to exclude accessions from below. They are the "cocktail set". From their example, this writer may add, drinking has spread out through both middle classes recently, and now includes about 72% of the total population.

The Upper-Middle, 10% out of 100, value health, talent, money; they have moral values in their drinking; they acknowledge restraining influences; most of the men drink on social occasions, but drinking by women is not quite general. This group has large influence in public affairs.

The Lower-Middle are 28% of the total—respectable people who do not have much money. This is where most of the taboos against drinking are to be found.

The Upper-Lower stratum contains 33% of the population; the labor and nationality groups. They have occupational restrictions against drunkenness and "excess", as a matter of course rather than social custom. They have no taboos regarding drink.

The Lower-Lower group, 25%, drink without restraint. Saturday night to Monday morning may be a weekend binge; both men and women

2. John Dollard, "Alcohol, Science and Society", *Yale Lectures,* 97-101.

drink; arrests for drunkenness, aggression while drunk and chronic drunkenness are common.

Beginnings of Dependence

The anesthetic pleasure that alcohol gives is learned usually at ages twelve to seventeen just as the needs of youth for socializing are keenest. The first experience may be in the home; or it may be in a peer group, to avoid the embarrassment of being different, not a "good mixer". Obviously these are not unhealthful motives. But after continuing trials, particularly if regular, a feeling of need begins to grow—a need to be free from frustration, fear, to feel again the sense of elation, self-confidence that light intoxication gives. As these psychological symptoms recur, this need grows stronger. The second stage is being reached. Depending on alcohol to obtain satisfactions is the danger line. When alcohol is most needed, it begins to be most dangerous; when not needed it is a "pleasure drug" with vaguest of vague limitations—a depressing drug administered, not by a doctor, but by a social situation. The social group is the activating agency far more than can be known, because of persistent effort to keep out of sight. Thus alcoholism begins to come into the lives of millions, out of their need to have friends and to be friendly.

Social Customs and Responsibility

The drink customs accepted by those who extol them as a privilege, *without concern* for their spread and consequences, are outstanding in modern culture, at all social levels. They are a direct source of most of the ills that come from alcoholic use. A unique illustration of this influence, when it comes from an upper social class, parallels the increasing trend toward drinking today.[3]

An old New New England family of wealth and prestige was noted for three generations for an outstanding adherance to non-alcohol culture, for influential abstinence and service, and for generous support of the anti-alcohol movements of a century. In the social group changes that have been occurring during the last few years, the head of the family, a Harvard graduate, continued his stand for abstinence. The wife and mother, from another high-prestige family, now provides alcoholic drinks for their many social affairs and has raised the daughters to be drinkers. The cult of liquor prestige has outweighed in this family the influence

3. A long-time instance seen by the writer.

of both the religion and the wealth in their family traditions by the acceptance of the women of the family.

Is it not, then, a fundamental part of "The New Approach", when studying "the Problems of Alcohol" as we find them today, that there should be included an objective and critical analysis of the responsibilities of these prestige groups? How about their influence as a source of the patterns on drinking that dominate much of current society? Also, their concern—rather lack of concern—about the consequences of many of the patterns they set, and that are followed by the millions who, seeking to "keep up with the Joneses", turn in to the public a never-ending tread of heavy drinkers as well as alcoholics?

And is it not also a fundamental part of whole-problem thinking, to recognize as never before, the opportunity that these same "men and women of prestige and social culture" have to support the patterns and trends that lead toward the reduction of the power of the "drink cult" at the top? Accept the responsibility of the "cocktail hour"? Why not evaluate these customs in the light of scientific knowledge? Of social psychology? Of the lives of the un-thinking who, consciously or unconsciously, follow "upper set". Why not analyze realistically and debunk the welter of literary tradition, and massive advertising that exalt the various stages of intoxication?

The Social Sifting Process

In all frequent-drinking communities, a sifting process is going on. Steadily, the youth of the group who are nervously deficient, frustrated, filled with fears and inferiorities, or neglected by parents, and many others, with any "peculiar temperament" that is susceptible to alcohol, are initiated into drinking habits under which alcohol becomes a necessity to them. They are led to depend upon it before they have learned that to them alcohol is doubly dangerous. These potential drunkards, found in every class, from Upper-Upper to Lower-Lower, and in between, are thus channelled by the assumptions of the alcohol cult into lives of active drunkenness.

With them go, through suggestion and example, others who do not, or cannot, or just don't want to keep their daily allowance below the danger line, that neither the scientists nor their own experience can define.

"Carriers" Of Alcoholic Sickness

Alcoholic illness may be regarded as contagious, in a social sense, at least. If so, how is it communicated? How does it reach those who are susceptible to it?

The common cold, the "flu", tuberculosis, and many fevers are spread by contact of people with each other; by air, water, the mosquito, other media. By identifying these "carriers" and isolating them, many sources of infection and sickness that were dangerously prevalent a generation or two ago, have been reduced, even eliminated. Typhoid, malaria, yellow fever are now subject to decisive reduction and control by sanitary measures. When the means by which they were spread had been determined, their suppression became possible. With advance in community sanitation and preventive health education, the corresponding "carriers" of alcoholism—although this sickness is in no sense a germ disease—may also be isolated, studied, identified, made non-toxic and eliminated.

Suggestion, invitation, and fashion are the starting and continuing factors for moderate and heavy drinking alike. Back of these, in some groups, stand the inherited traditions of alcoholic pleasure, the conventions, customs and ceremonials that make it seem essential to them. Almost automatically, under these assumptions, youth of all degrees of susceptibility to alcohol, "problem children" and those whose problems are no more severe than others in ordinary living, are exposed to the illusion of alcoholic satisfaction, learn to accept it, and find in it release from "whatever ails you".

The "carriers", therefore, of alcoholic illness are social drinkers and group approvals. These spread among all who are not conditioned against it, and are at all susceptible, the peculiar desire, that for many, in every generation, becomes dominant. The significant point, as Horton says, is "that there must be a social or cultural situation that provides the occasion and some degree of permission, before even the neurotic begins the process of becoming an alcoholic."

Social drinking sifts out of the total drinking group those who eventually become seriously alcoholic, whether they are neurotic or are ordinarily able to take it, with little or no unfortunate results.

What the germ-laden air of a crowded streetcar, or the fly, or the mosquito, or contaminated water are to other infections, drinking customs in analogy, are to alcoholism, and to the milder stages of intoxication that precede it.

In infantile paralysis, there is evidence that healthy "carriers", people who are not themselves sick, play a part in spreading the disease to which they are themselves resistant. So, in alcoholism, the initiation of the illness may, and often does, come from those who themselves resist excess and are proud of it, the influential, moderate drinkers.

For it is he—or she—the social drinker of "distinction", not the inebriate or the alcoholic, who stands out as the ideal of the youthful beginner and the long-time habitual drinker alike.

Continuing Pressure of Economic Interests

The pressure of economic interest in the production and sale of alcoholic drink tends constantly to increase both the quantity and frequency of drinking beyond any normal demand that may prevail in a community where the custom is generally accepted. This is a background of great significance that cannot well be ignored.

The desire for alcoholic experience, once a habit has been established and dependence created, brings with it a sense of need that is insistent—increasingly insistent in its call for satisfaction, from mild degrees of pleasure to heavy drinking and inebriety, if not held in severe personal, group, and public control. Factors that differentiate the liquor industry from those of other industries are recognized throughout civilization, not only because of the danger of immediate excess, but also because of the increasing economic opportunity to capitalize on the profits from excessive consumption and the increasing drug desire. At the end of the greatest sociological experiment ever made to control this force—the drastic attempt of America to remove it entirely by Prohibition—a nationally known legal and civic writer said: "The private profit motive by which sales are artificially stimulated is the greatest single contributing cause of the evils of excess."[4]

The fact that a commercial product available to everyone, is ready to supply unlimited quantities of a brain-depressing article for pleasure purposes—one that leaves extra heavy burdens of the community—cannot be ignored as a factor in the economy of a people.

To underestimate the promotional power of organized liquor is unrealistic. To its advertising, economic, and political appeals the public

---

4. Raymond B. Fosdick and Albert Scott, *Toward Liquor Control,* 1933, p 91.

must become intelligent, not gullible. For the depressing effects of alcohol make the business in it an exploitation of human tensions, fears, inferiorities and excesses.

The culture of America that centers in alcohol should be more critically understood, brought to public attention for what scientific understanding shows it to be. Widespread and popular, it is highly prized among the social elite, in ceremonials in Washington, New York, Hollywood, and, consequently, by the millions and millions of aspiring imitators, "social climbers" in the middle classes who are the main body of the American people.

From alcoholic sociability there comes a constant stream of drunkenness, of lesser and greater degree, and a final stream of inebriated humanity. Since the initiating and guiding sources are social and economic, social customs must be faced as a basic part of any movement to solve the problems resulting.

The specific desire for alcohol is created anew in each generation. The custom of using it is initiated among youth and continued by social approval, the attitudes of groups and trade promotion. The specific desire for it comes into existence after contact with alcohol itself, after the experience of each individual with the sort of sensations that it yields. There is no natural desire for it as a compelling motive; drink desires are not merely artificial; they also replace desires that have been diverted from healthy satisfaction by the tradition of alcoholic pleasure. Thus, their source, expression, and consequences are different basically from the gratifications of the human need for food, clothing, recreation, companionship. Their unfortunate results and excesses are the outgrowth of illusion, not of abuse, not of intemperance. The alcohol problem is not properly a "temperance question" at all. It is an anesthetic (or narcotic) drug problem. And being social in origin and pressure for continuance, all constructive efforts to mitigate the consequences of "drink" should take these social origins into account.

Chapter XIV

SOCIAL TRADITIONS, MORES AND NEVER-ENDING IDEALISM

A New Beginning

ALL THE WAY UP THE TRAIL, since man became man, at all stages, we find vivid stories of both the pleasures and the tragic sufferings that have been coming from intoxication, mild, moderate and wildly drunken into human living. And the variety and forms of ease and relief—or of habitual excess and devastation—have continued to increase in complexity and range, as society has refined and commercialized the various forms of beverages that have carried intoxication into daily living.

A pleasure substance—sometimes a food, or so it seemed to be—a "Gift of the God", it was and has remained, from the childhood days of the human race into the present era of space-travel inventiveness that has not yet found an adequate solution. Yet during all these years, due to the characteristic appeal of this popular drug, alcohol, and the persistent desire of men for its effects, in mild or heavy degrees or drunkenness, it has been rejected by a high minority in every generation that has observed and was at all concerned.

A Culture and a Counter Culture

The emotional experience of a group drinking together in the later centuries and today, are not greatly different from those of a primitive group around a forest fire, with sober guards to signal the coming of an enemy tribe, or the antics of a teen-age group returning from a party with a sober driver. Even a group of businessmen at a convention or get-together of old alumni grads are not reluctant to having a few of their number remain sober, or relatively so, as a safety squad. Multiple practice through the centuries have given such practices the standing of a cult in the culture of much modern living.

But to be realistic, it must not be overlooked that this theme of toxic enjoyment, of light to serious anesthesia, has always been accompanied by a counter theme of warning from keen observers. Continuous excess and degrading trends toward disaster began to appear among serious number of those who "took too much", or too frequently. They saw these trends as increasing dangers to themselves and heavy burdens in the community. Thus, there has been at all ages a culture of complete non-use, and one of heavily restricted use, among those who saw and understood. Their criticism has often been sharp, drastic, yet very realistic. They have denounced "liquor" often with little discrimination, hoping to shut off beginnings of drunkenness, crime and disorder. Back of the historical cult of "drink" there had come a never-ending wail of sorrow, excess, misery and inhumanity to men that is seen wherever alcoholic culture prevails.

Both history and recent scientific research now make it clear that serious disorders and alcoholism come from every walk of life; that people of an immature, undeveloped personality, the young, the overly sensitive, the youth from unhappy homes where parents have been very possessive or dictatorial, are the first to become habituated to the drug alcohol. From such groups come approximately 5,000,000 American people who have drink disordered lives. To this estimate made by Dr. E. N. Jellinek, of the noted Yale Center of Alcohol Studies and the World Health Organization, it must be added, as stated by Dr. Jellinek, that "anyone", however free from personality defects, may become an alcoholic—and many, many do—one out of every ten to eighteen who begins drinking—a total that cannot be definitely determined because of complicating influences. Regular and heavy drinking lead to this condition. Dr. Jellinek and others thus estimate that up to 50% of all Americans who reach this stage do so mainly because of social drinking.

In seeking to clarify further this aspect of the problem, Dr. Marvin A. Brock, of the Committee on Alcoholism of the American Medical Association, after special research relating to "Teen-age Drinking" reports that "any youth, if he drinks for the effects it gives, for the courage he needs and without which he cannot face problems, then indeed alcohol is no longer a beverage, but a drug to give him something artificially he does not himself possess."

But what of the large number who do drink for some form of effect? Who have little or no instability? Or a known emotional disorder? Those who have grown up into the atmosphere of frank social acceptance of alcohol as a normal way of life, yet have become frequent users or dependent to some degree of intoxication to enable them to carry on their daily activities—the point at which alcoholism is now scientifically recognized as having its beginning—the line at which one out of every ten to eighteen may definitely be an alcoholic, "a sick man"?

Divergent Trend

For many years, particularly the last one hundred and fifty in America and Northern Europe, two very divergent trends have been outstanding and persistent in social culture relating to the use of alcohol. Each has created and left deep markings in the attitudes, philosophies and practices of the people of these countries notwithstanding substantial changes in popular support at different periods.

First, there is the understanding that accepts the drink culture and social patterns of the past as having continuing value for the present and future, with little or no critical attention to consequences, responsibility or need for serious improvements.

Second, there have always been those who are deeply concerned—who resist the cult of drink, seek strong personal and social control or discard it wholly in personal practice of abstinence. They accept responsibility and are ready to set aside their own use when to do so "would help to clean up the neighborhood."

There are distressed personalities in the non-drinking culture of ours. But they do not—cannot—become alcoholics until alcohol has been added to their neurosis. A disturbed person who never drinks will remain a disturbed person. Only when he accepts drink, in effect joins the alcohol cult, can he become an alcoholic. It is absurd to call anyone an "alcoholic" who never took an intoxicating drink.

The active factor that adds alcoholism to neurosis comes from cultural environment. As explained by Dr. John Dollard, anthropologist at Yale, "there must be a social and cultural situation which provides occasion and some degree of permission before a neurotic can even begin the process of becoming an alcoholic."

The problems of alcohol have now taken on new meaning. There is new questioning. Study and research must now be on wider grounds than when this problem was regarded as mainly personal. To recognize and study the two-directional trends in alcoholic culture requires the examination of social sources, motivations, and objective evaluation of the cult of pleasure drinking itself.

The unfortunate sequences of the drinking cult do not and cannot be limited to the drinker, social or "moderate", and his local group. They spread out through the community; they affect the lives of all in direct and indirect contact with the drinking group; they influence the standards of the far-reaching, persistent, and great, if not inevitable. In extent the casualties of heavy drinking, the creation of alcohol addicts, the deterioration of the 5,500,000 citizens who become inebriates, is a national tragedy equivalent to a war of nations.

The custom of social drinkers thus comes into question as closely related to the initiating and cultural atmosphere in which much alcoholism begins.

This aspect of the problem, *responsibility,* must now be taken into account as deeply significant. It has been overlooked or minimized in both the "Temperance movement" and in the alcoholism emphases of recent years.

The problem is now one of mass drug satisfaction, correlated closely with dependence on a questionable drug for the happiness which all men seek, and with tendencies that make it "one of the greatest social questions of today." It is aggravated at one extreme by the powerful but childish pressure in polite society "to keep up with the Jones", and complicated at another by the dramatic exhibitionism of teen-age auto parties on their way home after a drinking party. "The Alcoholic" is thus not the whole, nor the most significant, part of the whole question. Mental, emotional, public health, ethical and religious motives and consequences demand new and additional research and action on what we already know. "The Nectar of the Gods", has not yet been freed from its reputation as "A Work of the Devil".

For, as Lecomte du Nouy, Harvard philosopher and sociologist, has said, the road of "progress toward solving such problems requires far-reaching changes in cultural attitudes as well as scientific understanding and long-time programs. These can be made."

Science cannot solve the Alcohol problem. Science can help. Science alone cannot do it, only you, the public, can do it. There is enough scientific knowledge already stored in university libraries to do it, if gotten out to the public and used, was a theme in the first lectures at the first Yale School of Alcohol Studies in 1943.

Ambivalence in the Custom

The various and often conflicting satisfactions thus deeply set in drinking culture are explained by Dr. Abraham Meyerson, Harvard sociologist and medical expert, who says that "alcohol is the drug that is used to enhance fellowship and evince gaiety, celebration and economy. It is not simply a drug of escape and oblivion, but also one of the celebration and ceremony." He shows that society "extols and builds up the manufacture and sale into a major industry, exerting great propaganda power, encouraging its use . . . synonymous with sociability . . . extolling the capacity to drink. On the other hand, it punishes, mocks and derides the alcoholic, . . . a stock source of humor is the drunkard or the man under the influence of alcohol."

One third of our total population is fully alcoholic, one third non-alcoholic; and one third seriously questions the cult even while participating in it.

Thus society as a whole, both wants and rejects alcohol. "This," says Dr. Meyerson, "is outstanding in early and modern culture; it occurs even in drinking groups." There are no such mixed attitudes toward the use of any other drug so far as Western Civilization is concerned.

Major Responsibility

To the large majority who accept and practice drink customs alcohol is important, socially and economically. This section includes moderates, regular and compulsive users; those who are interested in the industry; government officers who raise taxes; and all who by prestige and social approval constitute the 65% to 75% or more who are generally classified as drinkers. They support drink culture with little or no regard to its questionable aspects. Among them are the men and women who have had serious experiences with the problems.

The non-drinkers, 35% or more, constitute a very substantial and persistent minority that rejects alcohol as a beverage. They regard it as a source of mental and emotional disorder and of personal and potential danger in the community. This clear-cut section is found parallel to the drink section wherever and whenever drinking prevails in the culture of a people.

The beverage use of the drug alcohol is beyond all question more prevalent and excessive, in social consequences than is the use of all similar drugs combined.

Is it reasonable to expect, therefore, that the spreading and deepening trends toward the anesthesia of alcohol go on unrestrained without a corresponding increase in the number of addicts? Can the environment out of which modern alcoholism comes by the millions be improved? Can "alcoholic sickness" be reduced—then eliminated as tuberculosis and other diseases are now being conquered by medical science? Can drunken driving, petty and major crime, the liquor share in juvenile delinquency, in slum life, be substantially reduced while mild degrees of intoxication—to say nothing of the heavier—retain the dominant but thoughtless and irresponsible approval of the 65% of public practice and opinion they now possess?

How can education toward restraint and control, toward the growth of dependence on recreation, music, religion as normal release from the frustrations and serious ills of life be fully effective, stand out as normal and healthful as long as prestige use and access to intoxication is so easy? So suggestive? So commercially promoted? So unquestionably accepted by half or more of North American peoples?

The Approach of Maturity

The problems of alcohol have now taken on new meaning; there is renewed questioning. Study and research must now be on wider grounds than when this problem was regarded as purely personal. To recognize and study the two-directional trends in alcoholic culture requires the examination of social sources, motivations, and objective evaluation of the cult of pleasure drinking itself.

The unfortunate sequences of the drinking cult do not and cannot be limited to the drinker, social or "moderate", and his local group. They spread out through the community; they affect the lives of all in direct and indirect contact with the drinking group; they influence the standards of the society of which they are a part. These unavoidable sequences are far reaching, persistent and great, if not inevitable. In extent, the casualties of heavy drinking and drunkenness, the creation of alcohol addicts in the nation; the deterioration of the 5,000,000 citizens who become inebriates, is a national tragedy equivalent to a war of nations. The polite custom of friendly social drinking thus comes into question as closely related to the initiating and cultural atmosphere in which most alcoholism begins.

This aspect of the alcohol problem, responsibility, should now be taken into account as most significant. It has been overlooked or minimized in both the "temperance movement" and in "the alcoholic" and alcoholism emphases of recent years.

The problem is now of mass drug satisfaction, correlated closely and unavoidably with mass dependence by millions on a questionable drug for the happiness which healthful living gives. This use of the drug alcohol is beyond all question more prevalent, excessive, and worse in social consequences than is the use of all other drugs combined.

Is it reasonable to expect, therefore, that to be temperate can become a basic philosophy under these realistic conditions? Is it possible? Can the spreading and deepening trends toward the anesthesia of alcohol go on unrestrained without a corresponding increase in the number of addicts? Can the environment out of which modern alcoholism comes by the millions be improved? Can "alcoholic sickness" be reduced—then eliminated as yellow fever, malaria, and diptheria were eliminated years ago? As tuberculosis and other diseases are now being conquered by medical science? Can drunken driving, petty and major crime, the liquor share in juvenile delinquency, in slum life be substantially reduced while mild degrees of intoxication—to say nothing of the heavier—retain the dominant but thoughtless and irresponsible approval of the 65% of public practice and opinion they now possess?

How can education toward restraint and control, toward the growth of dependence on recreation, music, religion, as normal release from the frustrations and serious ills of life be fully effective, stand out as normal and healthful as long as prestige use and access to intoxicants is so easy? So suggestive? So commercially promoted? So unquestionably accepted by half or more of North American peoples?

Neither the history of drug pleasure, nor recent experience, nor scientific knowledge give much hope that this can be done without frankly questioning the tradition of social drink and the modern economic promotion regarding the part they play as dynamic sources of the too-well known excesses. These sources should now be studied, recognized for what they are, for steps that may be taken toward improvement—by all who help initiate solution of the problems of alcohol—toward prevention of alcoholism and its end-product, the Alcoholic. These sources as well as the nervous disorders and emotional immunity that mark the potential alcoholic are basic factors that should no longer be ignored in this last half of the twentieth century.

A Confident New Beginning

The knowledge that scientific research, history, and human observation together reveal, shows clearly that this problem must be undertaken from many different approaches. No one attitude, objective, or field of service is enough if operating alone. The curative, by the doctor, counselor, minister; the rehabilitative, by the A.A., the Salvation Army, and the psychiatrist; the industrial relations program in the factory that seeks to recover high-grade employees from alcoholism; the restoration of neglected neighborhoods to head off juvenile delinquency; personal counseling by religious, medical, psychiatric and welfare experts with youth and those who have alcohol problems; basic preventive and never-ending education of parents and their children; objective scientific education in the schools; more vitalized education in the home and church, especially among young adults—the parents and social leaders; increasing instruction in colleges on all aspects of the problem, particularly in psychology, sociology, personal and public health, and government; student group discussion in preparation for service and citizen leadership; active participation by all citizens in the never-ending struggles in civic, social, municipal, state, and national politics that have to do with public opinion; and effective legal control or final banishment of alcohol as a dangerous drug, as other drugs of similar character are treated. These many approaches are now necessary if "the fourth greatest illness" that effects humanity is to be substantially reduced or eliminated.

Both immediate and long-range programs are now imperative. Resources in experience and scientific research are now more abundant than ever before. A constructive approach, broad enough, deep enough, continuous enough, and of long enough range to undermine all the known sources of alcoholism—personal, social, economic—and its degrading consequences in human living, may now have a confident beginning —a far more confident beginning than at any previous time in the century of experimentation. For those experiments have brought out both the size of the job and the necessity of doing it.

Chapter XV

CONCERN, OPPORTUNITY AND THE FUTURE

The spirit of adventurous service as it appears in the upper college and graduate years of many of us, to give a few volunteer—even sacrificial—years to an idealistic field of human need, or a lifetime, lives on today as in 1900 and all the years between.

Just two weeks before this page was first written, 42 graduates from various colleges finished ten weeks of special training at a large university for the Peace Corps. Ten days later, they were on their way to join other students sent out the previous year to share with natives in developing the new independent Federal Republic of the Cameroons. Thousands have followed since—to all parts of the world.

From the Intercollegiate School of Alcohol Studies at McMaster University, a week or two earlier, 43 students and instructors of Canada and the United States returned to college with a deeper understanding and a new sense of devotion to giving creative service as citizens toward reducing the tragedies of alcohol and alcoholism in North America. They were prepared to give similar devotion to this world problem of alcohol, which continues to keep in our culture between 5,000,000 and 5,500,000 alcoholics and inebriates.

While this page was being revised in 1964, 400 or more students and recent graduates were completing training under qualified leaders at several colleges in preparation for volunteer service in the Equal Rights movement that was gripping the attention of the nation that year. They were learning how to share with citizens, black and white, as equal American citizens. By the same date, over 6,000 Peace Corps volunteers were at work in 46 countries around the world, many of them for years of continual service.

Realistically, after 150 years of experimentation, after great surges of public sentiment that demanded reform were followed by opposite surges toward loosened control and drunkenness, the problem of alcohol is here in force, as complicated as ever in history, obvious, obtrusive.

The excesses of drink are more concealed, but are still outstanding. The spread of social drinking is increasing; the cocktail hour is a social must.

The initiating of drink habits at ages 13 to 15 goes on unchecked. The transfer of drinkers into alcoholics is aided, not retarded, by social custom. Jails are crowded with repeating drunks; emotional and mental disturbances associated with alcohol are increasing. The heavy reality of the "alcoholic sick" is a gigantic fact in public health. The cost to industry from lost time and in taxes to the public in caring for drunkenness is never ending. These trends make the beverage alcohol problem one of supreme importance.

As individuals and groups come to depend upon alcohol for the various types of "joy" it gives, the number of those who ultimately become victims—addicts and heavy drinkers—will also increase. Irresponsible drinking and its consequences have been cumulative in the past; there is little reason to believe that this will not happen again, unless the "cult of 'drink'" is more effectively controlled than it has been in the past—or is at present.

The Alcoholic Sick Today

Then why not deeper concern and more neighborly aid and friendship for the alcoholic and his family, her family—symbol of this problem today? How shall we face their deep emotional disorders? These men and women all about us, outstanding victims of this gigantic health problem? What do we mean by these questions? Or do we know what we mean? Do we have a concern to know? What are the consequences of alcohol in our social and national life?

How far have we gone when we, the public, study the specifics above—the illness called "alcoholism", "temperance", "moderation", the heavy drinker", "the abstainer", "the tranquilizing drug", "this gift of the Gods", "drunkenness", "the addict"—questions that each wants to, and must, decide for himself. Or does he? "Where do the serious questions arise, or do they?"

Or the unanswered scientific question, "Is alcoholism a sickness, a sin, an emotional disorder, or what? Cause or consequence, or both? Why concern ourselves with it anyhow, and who does? Or should?

As an approach for study and research, may we not think of what it could mean if alcoholism should be seriously regarded by the public as an illness? If it should be treated wholeheartedly by medical and psychiatric experts with the knowledge and experience that they have gained in the reduction of other health disorders.

Modern medicine is working miracles. In just twenty years, polio has declined 90%; tuberculosis, 86%; appendicitis, 81%; influenza, the "flu" 93%; maternal deaths, 86%; acute rhematic fever, 87%. "A child born today can expect to live seven years longer than one born just 20 years ago," reports the president elect of the American Medical Association, Dr. Norman A. Welch, in *Today's Health,* June, 1964. Why not a parallel reduction instead of an increase in alcoholism?

Limitations to the Health Approach

The "Challenge of Good Health" to the constructive and basic progress that can be made in understanding and education is bound by limitations that do not obtain the full and free use of scientific research and knowledge such as has been available in fighting the diseases that have been so miraculously reduced in modern years.

As Abraham Meyerson, M.D., states: "It must be taken into account that the social attitude toward the drinking of alcohol is one of the most important things in our civilization . . . the whole attitude of society toward the use of alcohol and the alcoholic has become decidedly ambivalent."

The influence of the social patterns set by those who extol as a privilege, *without concern as to consequences,* the traditional drink customs of society came strongly to some of us at the first Yale School of Alcohol Studies in 1943—and ever since. Here there seemed to be a job for much further research. I continued to gain this impression as I attended the second school and five successive refresher conferences. The traditions and practices of the past seemed to me to be sources of alcoholic excess, basic sources into which most who become alcoholics had been born, or lived as children; those with individual instability could not escape; those most susceptible would become dependent on alcohol before they could know what was happening.

First, customs and sanctions spread out from prestige groups by invitation to all who seek to climb to similar positions of influence. Broadcast nightly to the millions and millions over television and radio, movies and glamorous trade advertising, drink culture becomes a vast sifting process that initiates, then keeps many who count on it for personal and for party entertainment, until, without knowledge of what is happening, a sense of dependence, then addiction has been created.

Second, economic interests arise at once in resistence when even well-tested scientific research brings out information that, if given publicity and application, would tend to reduce profits. A recent illustration was what happened when the report of a long time scientific research came relating to cigarette smoking and lung cancer and was given publicity. Such research reports relating to drunkenness have been given many times in past years but even more freely ignored by the public and even by the medical and health professions.

The Approach of Maturity

After 65 years of study and observation, it seems clear to this writer that the problems of alcohol come more from the age-old cult of irresponsible drinking than either the individual or the bottle. Certainly, there are enough stimulants such as coffee available everywhere from which to gain a pleasing sensation, and enough safe tranquilizers in drugstore windows from which to choose a means to escape from frustration and minor emotional disorders, without depending on the anesthesia of intoxication and inflicting on life companions and society the tragedies of drunkenness that mark our present alcoholic culture. A new sense of democratic responsibility is needed by our drinking majority.

As long as there are 5,000,000 deteriorating personalities in our everyday culture called "alcoholics", sick-people, by specialists, the fourth greatest health problem of today with its sources deeply related to the social traditions in which we live and as many deaths on the highways attributed to drinking pedestrians and drivers, there is occasion for serious concern. Study of this situation is needed by thinking younger people—college students as well as the general public. They are responding generously to other critical issues of the day, civil rights, racism, and the frictions between the new nations and the older ones that challenge all citizens, as does alcoholism these days of rugged world problems.

If there is a solution, we must continue to seek it. If *there are solutions,* they should *all* be given serious study by all younger citizens who will have to deal with them very soon.They must be studied objectively from backgrounds of scientific, experimental, and historical understanding; but with a sense of concern, for this social disorder is misunderstood, notwithstanding the accumulated scientific and experimental knowledge now available. Too few are concerned enough to seek a real understanding.

Practical Idealism

Briefly, one third of our total population today is fully alcoholic, one third non-alcoholic, and the other third questions the cult even while participating in it.

Modern research has made it certain that alcoholics come from every walk of life, that people of unstable personalities are the first to become heavy or compulsive drinkers—the emotionally unstable, the disordered, the immature, children from broken homes—youths whose parents have been cruel, overly possessive or dictatorial. From this source comes 40% or more of our 5,000,000 heavy drinkers and alcoholics.

But anyone, however free from personality defects, may become an alcoholic. Regular and heavy drinking lead to this condition. Dr. E. N. Jellinek, founder of the Yale School of Alcohol Studies and later a member of the World Health Organization, estimated that up to 60% of American alcoholics reached this stage mainly out of social drinking.

The larger problem is social and moral, not just one of mental and physical health, basic as these are to the total problem of alcohol. Neither personal abstinence alone, nor rehabilatation of the alcoholic alone can solve it. The more fundamental changes to be made will require the acceptance of a realistic sense of democratic responsibility, for more concern, and for participation of all clear-thinking citizens in the struggle to reduce alcoholism at its sources. Surely this is not too much to expect.

A Confident New Beginning

The knowledge that scientific research, history, and human observation together reveal clearly is that the problem must be undertaken from many different approaches. No one attitude or objective field of service is enough if operating alone. The *curative,* by the doctor, counselor, minister; the *rehabilitative,* by the A.A., the Salvation Army, and the psychiatrist; the industrial relations program in the factory that seeks to recover *highgrade employees* from alcoholism; the restoration of neglected neighborhoods to head off *juvenile delinquency;* personal counseling by religious, medical, psychiatric and welfare experts with *youth* and *those who have alcohol* problems; basic preventive and never-ending education of parents and their children; objective *scientific education* in the schools; more *vitalized education* in the home and church, especially among young adults—the parents and social leaders; increasing *instruction* in colleges on all aspects of the problem, particularly in psychology, sociology, personal and public health, and government; *student group discussion* in preparation for service and citizen leadership; active *participation* by all citizens in the never-ending struggles in civic, social, municipal, state, and national *politics* that have to do with public opinion; and effective *legal control* of alcohol as a dangerous drug, as other drugs of similar character must be controlled. These *many* approaches are now necessary if "the fourth greatest illness" that affects humanity is to be substantially reduced.

Both immediate and long-range programs are now imperative. Resources in experience and scientific research are more abundant than ever before. A constructive approach, broad enough, deep enough, continuous enough, and of wide enough range to undermine all the known sources of alcoholism—personal, social, economic—and its degrading consequences in human living, may now have a confident beginning—a far more confident beginning than at any previous time in the century of experimentation that has passed. For the many experiments made have brought out both the size of the job and the necessity of doing it.